# The Practice of
# Problem-Based Learning

BS ⇒ know
M ⇒ apply
D ⇒ think & create

Group project allows joint development
of a research question

# The Practice of
# Problem-Based Learning
## *A Guide to Implementing PBL*
## *in the College Classroom*

José A. Amador
Libby Miles
C. B. Peters
*University of Rhode Island*

ANKER PUBLISHING COMPANY, INC.
Bolton, Massachusetts

**The Practice of Problem-Based Learning**
*A Guide to Implementing PBL in the College Classroom*

ISBN 978-1-933371-07-8

Composition by Becky Arrants
Cover design by Karen Stroman

Anker Publishing Company, Inc.
563 Main Street
P.O. Box 249
Bolton, MA 01740-0249 USA

www.ankerpub.com

Library of Congress Cataloging-in-Publication Data

Amador, José A.
  The practice of problem-based learning : a guide to implementing PBL in the college classroom / José A. Amador, Libby Miles, C. B. Peters.
     p. cm.
  Includes bibliographical references and index.
  ISBN-13: 978-1-933371-07-8
  1. Problem-based learning. 2. Education, Higher. I. Miles, Libby. II. Peters, C. B. III. Title.

  LB1027.42.A76 2006
  378.1'7—dc22

                                                      2006006129

# Table of Contents

# About the Authors

**José A. Amador** is professor of soil science and microbial ecology at the University of Rhode Island. He received his B.S. degree (1982) in biochemistry, and M.S. (1986) and Ph.D. (1990) degrees in soil microbiology from Cornell University. José has been at the University of Rhode Island since 1992, where he teaches in the Department of Natural Resources Science and the Honors Program. For the past six years, he has used the problem-based learning approach to teach courses in introductory soil science, soil microbiology, soil and water chemistry, and land use. His research focuses on the applications of soil ecology and microbiology to problems in nutrient cycling, wastewater disposal, bioremediation, and plant nutrition.

**Libby Miles** is associate professor in the College Writing Program at the University of Rhode Island. She received her B.A. degree in theatre from Williams College (1986), and M.A. (1995) and Ph.D. (1999) degrees in rhetoric and composition from Purdue University. Libby has been at the University of Rhode Island since 1998, where she has taught in the college writing program, the English department's graduate program, and the honors program. She also directed the university's writing center. She has used problem-based learning in several of her writing classes, from

Honors Writing for First-Year Students, to Business Communications, to a graduate seminar in Rhetoric and Institutional Critique. Her current research interests are the economic and institutional conditions of writing and writing instruction, rhetoric as an agent of social change, and interdisciplinary writing.

 **C. B. Peters** is professor of sociology at the University of Rhode Island. He received his B.A. degree (1971) from Westmont College, and M.A. (1973) and Ph.D. (1977) degrees from the University of Kentucky. His scholarly expertise is in cultural sociology and the sociology of knowledge. In addition to his sociological books and articles, C.B. has published papers and presented workshops and seminars on teaching and instructional design. He has used problem-based learning units with first-year students in large enrollment sections of introductory sociology.

# Foreword

As director of the Instructional Development Program at the University of Rhode Island, I spend most of my days talking with faculty about what they hope students will learn in their courses and how they might design instruction to ensure that learning occurs. Many faculty are concerned about two aspects of student learning. First, they want their students to acquire the knowledge and skills necessary to address the major questions and problems of their disciplines. Second, they want their students to have the ability and interest to continue learning beyond the duration of specific courses. These conversations with faculty often turn to problem-based learning (PBL), an approach that is especially well suited to these goals.

In brief, PBL begins by posing a complex, authentic problem, one which students might encounter in real life. Working in groups, students discuss three questions: What do we know? What else do we need to know? How will we learn it? Students then research the areas they've identified and return to the group for more discussion. They repeat the cycle until they solve or resolve the problem. This book offers a valuable introduction to this approach by describing PBL in rich detail.

In my conversations with faculty, first reactions to PBL vary. Some claim "I already do that. Whenever I introduce new material, I follow up with an exercise or assignment so students can apply the material." That's good practice, but it's not PBL. In PBL, the problem comes first and it drives learning, a point that is well emphasized in this book. It is this feature of PBL that resembles learning outside college classrooms and enables students to develop lifelong learning skills.

For many faculty considering PBL, content coverage is an immediate issue. "It sounds interesting, but our curriculum requires that I cover certain content, and this does not sound like a plan to do that." PBL does engage students in covering content, but out of a need to learn the content in order to solve or resolve a problem. The result is often increased motivation and deeper learning. This does not happen magically, of course. Content objectives must be built into the problem. That is easier said than done, but readers will find here some useful strategies for ensuring content learning is embedded in PBL problems.

Student expectations and reactions also worry faculty considering PBL. "I shudder to imagine what my students would say if I used this approach. They already grumble if I assign a task and do not demonstrate how to accomplish it or walk them through it step by step. If I were to give them a problem and turn them loose to determine what they need to learn and how they will learn it, I fear they would accuse me of shirking my teaching responsibilities." Such fears are not unfounded. Some students—especially those in early stages of cognitive development—react in exactly those ways, and they are not shy about expressing their reactions on student evaluations.

This book does not skirt issues related to the developmental level of students. The authors are clearly knowledgeable about student development research, and that knowledge informs both the issues they identify and the advice they offer. *Should we use PBL throughout the course or ease students into it, perhaps with only one or two PBL units? What should the course syllabus say about PBL—about readings, assignments, due dates, and the like? How much structure should PBL problems provide? How much guidance must the instructor offer? How do we ensure that groups work productively? Does class size matter?* The authors speak from experiences in different disciplines with students at different developmental levels in classes of different sizes. The result is a book you can trust.

*The Practice of Problem-Based Learning* combines a conversational tone with individual commentary and group reflection. The advice and recommendations offered make this an excellent resource for faculty considering PBL as well as for those already experimenting with the approach.

*Bette LaSere Erickson*
*Director, Instructional Development Program*
*University of Rhode Island*

# Preface

This book turned out to be an exercise in problem-based learning (PBL). We started with an authentic problem—writing a "how to" guide to PBL for college faculty. Our small team of authors was composed of faculty from different disciplines, but all were experienced in using PBL at the college level. We were confident we knew plenty about PBL and writing books: We could do this. Of course, it wasn't long before we reached the limits of our knowledge and were trying to figure out what else we needed to know so we could move toward a solution to the problem of writing a book on PBL. Along the way we experienced many of the challenges (lead changes at various points, scheduling conflicts, disagreements), as well as the positive interdependence, associated with group dynamics in the PBL setting. The result, after working on this PBL problem for over a year (too long by our own standards, as you will see in Chapter 2), is our solution: a true group product.

This book responds to a movement in American higher education toward active learning, and a growing expectation that students be able to use information, not just acquire it. This emphasis on developing higher-order thinking and metacognitive skills in undergraduate education is taking place in the context of institutional mandates to articulate student learning outcomes. Into this scene comes PBL.

Initially implemented in professional schools (particularly in medicine and business) as a way to teach strategic access to and use of information rather than the traditional (and less effective) memorization model, PBL has since infused other fields of study as well. We, for example, teach within disciplines in humanities (Libby), social sciences (C.B.), and life sciences (José). PBL has been developed and promoted as an approach to teaching that encourages students to take responsibility for their own learning in sequenced problem solving through several phases. As a result, it has been embraced by a number of institutions on a wide scale, perhaps most notably the University of Delaware.

As we tried to introduce PBL into our courses, we realized that the information we sought (*How do you do this in a large class? How much PBL should I introduce in my course? How do I grade all of this? How do I deal with "hitchhikers"?*) was scattered among many different sources: edited collections, education journals and edited series, and web sites. These sources offered an eclectic mix of theory and practice that—although often useful—was difficult to sift through for us as interested—but uninitiated—PBL teachers. This book is our attempt to put together in one place the information that we wish we had had when we set out to use PBL.

*The Practice of Problem-Based Learning* provides a guide for the development and implementation of PBL in courses at the college level. It is written with usefulness in mind, providing hands-on guidance from real professors to real professors. The book assumes minimal familiarity with PBL and encourages instructors to build it into their classes as makes sense for their students and their own situation. We have tried to provide a coherent narrative perspective through collaborative writing. The book includes many examples of PBL in action through every stage of problem development and implementation. It also integrates cross-disciplinary experiences into the *doing* of PBL in the college classroom.

This book is written for faculty, graduate teaching assistants, and faculty development professionals. Its nuts and bolts approach makes it valuable to those interested in learning how to *do* PBL, as well as to those already doing PBL and who would like to learn more about what other practitioners do in their classrooms. Faculty development programs focused on improving undergraduate teaching through innovative methods to encourage active learning can use this book as a resource for faculty, as well as in workshop settings. Faculty teaching courses in higher education and teaching methods will find in this book a useful introduction to the practice of PBL.

# Acknowledgements

We thank Deborah Allen, of the University of Delaware, whose PBL workshops at the University of Rhode Island got us started. We also thank Bette LaSere Erickson and Glenn Erickson, of the University of Rhode Island's Instructional Development Program, for encouraging us to write this book. We are indebted to the many colleagues who, through discussions or by example, have helped us move toward an active learning approach: Jef Bratberg, Nancy Cook, Lynne Derbyshire, Jeremiah Dyehouse, Jeff Grabill, Josef Görres, Tom Husband, Valerie Karno, Roger LeBrun, Karen Markin, James Porter, Mark Schaub, Marie Schwartz, Robert Schwegler, Michele Simmons, Patricia Sullivan, and Kathleen Torrens. Finally, we thank our students, whose curiosity, energy, and enthusiasm made adoption of PBL in our courses worth the effort.

*José A. Amador*
*Libby Miles*
*C. B. Peters*
December 2005

# 1
# Why (We) Use PBL

C. B. Peters teaches Sociology 100 (General Sociology), a general education course, to more than 500 undergraduate students in a large auditorium.

C.B.:

*The first thing you'll notice is the noise. It is often difficult to hear yourself think, and conversing even with those close at hand takes persistence and a strong voice. Once you get used to the noise, you'll also notice the groups of students strewn throughout the auditorium: sitting in misshapen circles near the podium, propped up against the wall on the mezzanine, leaning every which way in the theater seats to see and hear one another.*

*You might be tempted to conclude that class had not yet started, that soon the instructor would arrive, quieting the din and sending the students scampering to their seats, notebooks in hand, ready to attend to the day's lecture. But amid the din and the sprawl you notice a figure—in fact, several of them—walking from group to group, occasionally crouching, listening, and then responding to what appear to be questions. Then there is the writing that is going on. In each cluster there is at least one student—sometimes more—who is busy writing on a goldenrod sheet. Sometimes the sheets are handed to the circulating figures who glance at them, nod, return them, comment, and move on.*

*It all seems more like a strange party or, perhaps, a demonstration of some kind, than what usually happens in a classroom. Your wondering is interrupted by the crackling of a microphone being switched on, and your attention is drawn to one of the figures who has been moving throughout the room. "If I could get your attention for just a minute," he begins. The room slowly quiets as he continues. "Many of you are trying to resolve this issue by making it only about gender, and many others are trying to do the same thing by making it only about religion. The reason this is such a difficult problem is that both things are in play."*

*At that, there is a small burst of noise as the clusters of students reinitiate their conversations. You can't hear much very clearly, but you do catch a few phrases from the students nearby. "See, that's what I was saying. You can't just say we should recognize his religion because she has a right, too." The figure with the microphone continues. "You'll need to come to some conclusions in the next 10 minutes or so because I want to spend a little time talking about the next part of our problem that you'll be working on for Friday's class."*

*In a few minutes, the goldenrod sheets, filled with writing, are collected by the circulating figures, as the man with the microphone on his tie concludes the day's activities. "So, given what your group said about this interaction between the woman and the real estate agent, what principles for public life in a good society can you articulate? Meet with each other, in person, by cell phone, by email, by messaging, however, between now and Friday. We'll collect your work then, give you some feedback on what you did today, and then move to the last part of the problem-based portion of our course."*

Libby Miles teaches HPR 112, Honors Study in Writing and Rhetoric, a first-year writing course, to 20 students. The course meets in a computer lab.

Libby:

> *If you were to walk into my classroom, you would not hear the typical sounds of productive work but instead the chatter of cell phone conversations, electronic beeps as instant messages pop up on computer screens around the room, and the tapping of keyboards and clicking of mice as students Ask Jeeves and Google and then exclaim "I found him!" and "Aw, I was soooo wrong!"*
>
> *Make no mistake; in a PBL writing classroom, this is work. And this is only the first day of class, about 15 minutes into the first session. For many of these first-year students, this is their first college class.*
>
> *Five minutes into their first day of class, students have only just learned the names of the other students in their four-person group. The professor has said very little, except to introduce the first problem—a fictitious internship with a local member of Congress, slated to begin during the next class session. The students' job today is to learn as much as they need about the representative with whom they will be working, using any of the resources available in the classroom. They begin with the knowledge they carry within themselves, pooling their understanding of the Congressman—a process that (much to their embarrassment) takes only a few minutes.*
>
> *Having quickly reached the limits of their own prior knowledge, students identify what they will need to know before showing up for the first day of the internship. What party does the Congressman belong to? How long has he been in office? What are his pet issues?*

*Who are his constituents, and how do they feel about him? What do others think of him? What is his stance on key issues the students might care about? With these questions in hand, the students turn to their own technologies: cell phones, instant messaging, and Google searches. Within 15 minutes, they have begun answering their own questions. A productive competitiveness infuses the class environment as students try to get answers before another group does (and at some point, eavesdropping becomes a highly developed form of research as well). After 30 minutes, all five groups have ample information and a sense of the context they will enter when they begin their internship the next day. Their homework will be to find answers to the rest of the questions, and compile a one-page fact sheet about the Congressman for the next class. Students usually begin dividing responsibilities and collaborating on their fact sheets without prompting.*

*With this, the basic PBL tools and processes for the class have been established, and student groups have begun to cohere. Having set the tone for the class, the professor is now free to present typical first-day fare: policies and the syllabus. Within the context of all the preceding activity, usually dry classroom logistics and policies seem more meaningful.*

José Amador teaches NRS 212, Introduction to Soil Science, to approximately 50 students in what might be described as a typical classroom.

José:

*Erin, a landscape architecture student, is arguing with Ryan, a wildlife conservation major, about soil. An hour ago, Erin, Ryan, and almost 50 of their fellow undergraduate students were sitting in the classroom on the first day of class, waiting for Introduction to Soil Science to start. The fact that it is a required course—on dirt—really makes for an inauspicious start to the semester. "What's there to know about dirt? This is going to be soooooo boring..." Yet there they are: Erin contends that only if you can grow plants in it can you call it soil, and Ryan argues that soil that once supported plant life, but no longer does because of contamination with heavy metals, should still be considered soil. "Besides"—chimes in Janet, a horticulture student—"if it's not considered soil, then regulations that govern remediation would not apply." This argument is taking place publicly, in class, in front of all of their classmates.*

*The source of the argument is a problem that involves drafting a definition of soil for the purposes of environmental regulation. When they go back to their groups to continue their discussions, the students decide that they need more information about the properties of soil, what constitutes soil contamination, and the existing regulations governing remediation. By the time they finish deciding who is going to do what, they realize that class has officially been over for at least five minutes.*

## Why We Switched

These situations are real. They took place in our classrooms, and are the consequence of a shift in teaching paradigm. The results have been rewarding, although the journey has been sometimes frustrating and fraught with anxiety. For some of us the shift has come about gradually, a sequence of adjustments in a broader range of student-centered teaching practices. For others, it has been almost an "instant makeover."

For us, the shift to problem-based learning (PBL) began with the realization that even the outstanding students in our courses were at a loss when faced with the need to remember and/or use the knowledge they had gained in class to solve an authentic problem or to extrapolate principles beyond the context of the classroom. The learning in our classrooms seemed to occur in isolation, and students were for the most part unable to make connections between what they knew and what it could be used for.

José:

> *This certainly is the case for me. Since I make an effort to involve undergraduate students in my research, this was something I observed every semester for about eight years: A student who on exams could describe in great detail the mechanism by which soil bacteria oxidized ammonium to nitrate, could not make the connection to the same processes as a source of nitrate in soil. Or, a student who had aced her general chemistry lab was unable to make a salt solution of a certain concentration. Eventually, once these students spent some time in the lab, asking questions, listening to discussions, reading, and trying things out, they began to make the connections between what they already knew and the things they were trying to understand in their undergraduate research projects. But the fact that it took even the brightest students weeks, sometimes months, to make the connection was troublesome.*
>
> *About five years ago, after attending a one-hour seminar on PBL, I made a radical change: I turned all of my courses into PBL courses. I burned my bridges— threw away my overheads and lecture notes—and I have not looked back since. The change has been remarkably positive for my students. And for me.*
>
> *To me, the learning that takes place as part of the PBL process is analogous to how our sense of direction*

*changes when we have to drive ourselves somewhere. If I*
*am a passenger in a car, I have a general idea of how*
*to get there. I can even get a very good feel for how to get*
*there. But even after many trips to the same place, I may*
*not be exactly sure of how far to go on Elm Street or at*
*which intersection to turn left. However, if I am the*
*driver, I learn the route in a much shorter time. I learn*
*the content (route) in the process of solving the problem*
*(trying to get to my destination). In PBL, you learn the*
*content because you need to do so in order to solve the*
*problem. This is just the opposite of what I did in my*
*lectures: I presented students with the facts and*
*principles and then asked them to apply them to solve*
*problems.*

The radical change to PBL paid off for José. Students in his
courses bring information learned in other courses into their
discussions, argue, ask substantive questions of each other, and even
question each other in public. The process is not always pretty, but
it is clear that learning is taking place.

Libby:

*In my field of rhetoric and composition, the move to*
*PBL can be a natural progression. In both our*
*pedagogies and in our scholarship, the field of rhetoric*
*values situations for writing, and many of us feel that*
*teaching writing is best done within social contexts*
*(including, but not limited to, academic writing).*
*Many writing classes at all levels of the curriculum place*
*students in different writing situations and ask them to*
*respond to the situation appropriately and effectively.*
*Having tried these situational approaches with good*
*success with first-year students through seniors, I signed*
*up for a PBL workshop at the University of Rhode*
*Island to see if PBL offered something significantly*
*different from what I had been teaching all along. What*

*I found was heartening. I was already most of the way there, but PBL shifted my framework just enough to show me how I could revise my own course design to teach my subject even more effectively. PBL offered a predictable yet infinitely flexible framework within which my students could explore—and act upon— situational issues appropriately addressed with writing.*

*What does this all mean in my writing classes? PBL has become the ideal first project, encapsulating and introducing all the elements I hope to teach and practice: collaborating, engaging in increasingly sophisticated research, integrating technologies, being aware of and sensitive to different audiences, inhabiting situation-based writing, negotiating complex and diverse perspectives on an issue, and acting through writing toward some sort of resolution. Beginning each semester with a PBL problem better enables my first-year writers to complete individual situation-based writing projects for the rest of the semester (and, I hope, throughout their writing lives).*

The change was relatively easy for Libby. Her courses were already rich in group work, the case method, and situational discussion. Nevertheless, her willingness to graft PBL onto a successful teaching strategy has transformed her classroom and her role as instructor. The result has been even more powerful learning.

C.B.:

*Large class instruction comes with a series of built-in barriers to engaging students: Auditoria have fixed seats; enrollments comprise first-year (and often first-semester) students who lack the foundations of a discipline; lecturing, the traditional method of instruction, also provides the security of control and, if done well, the rewards of an entertained and hopefully educated audience. Over the years, I have invested a great deal of energy in trying to adapt the most engaging teaching practices—small group discussion, case studies, and the like—to a large introductory course in sociology.*

*For several years, I thought those efforts had been successful, and that with a little tinkering here and there I could smooth out the rough places that remained. My course had students working in small groups that would form and reform depending on the serendipity of seating. We used writing-to-learn activities, had students draw cognitive maps, and even asked them to write examination items from time to time. The course was fun, it was engaging, and students were learning.*

*Yet I was concerned that we had not gone far enough. The thought came to me one day during the first week of class. I had used as a prompt for a writing-to-learn activity the opening line from Anne Tyler's* [2001] Back When We Were Grownups: *"Once upon a time, there was a woman who discovered she had turned into the wrong person." I asked students to think (and write) what they had to know in order to make sense of this rather unusual sentence. After a few minutes devoted to their thinking and writing, and after some comments from the bolder students (and there were many), I spent the rest of the hour explaining what I thought one needed to know in order to make sense of Tyler's beginning.*

*I was good at it; students seemed both entertained and educated, but they hadn't solved the problem for themselves. They had watched me solve it. As I thought, I realized this was a recurring pattern in my course. I would spend hours unearthing interesting problems that would require an engaged sociological imagination to solve, and then give my students just a 10- or 15-*

*minute taste of what doing sociology was like before finishing each one for them.*

*PBL offered me a way to keep my students engaged in the "doing" of sociology over an extended period. Because I think that's what introductory courses ought to do—get students to do the discipline, not merely know about it—PBL seemed an ideal adjustment for a course that was already problem rich.*

In some ways, C.B.'s adaptation of PBL resembles Libby's. His course had moved away from the traditional lecture format and he was committed to getting students involved. In other ways, however, launching PBL in a course with 500 students is always a radical change. So, like José's, C.B.'s classroom is not always pretty, but it is alive with learning.

## What Is PBL?

For the past decade some educators have promoted the value of PBL for learning across the curriculum. In their formulation, PBL involves small groups of students working in permanent groups to learn the course content within the framework of a realistic problem. The process involves the following (Boud & Feletti, 1997):

1. *Present students with a problem.* Students assess the problem and identify what they know in relation to the problem.

2. *Determine what aspects of the problem they do not understand.* These learning issues serve to focus group discussion.

3. *Rank learning issues in order of importance.* The group decides which issues will be considered by the whole group or by individuals. In the case of individual follow-up, that student is then responsible for informing the rest of the group about his or her findings.

4. *Explore previous learning issues and integrate new knowledge in the context of the problem.* Students summarize their progress,

make connections between previous and newly acquired knowledge, and develop new learning issues.

These steps are repeated until the group is satisfied that they have developed an acceptable solution to the problem.

We have structured this book to provide a general sense of, and our individual perspectives on, the practice of PBL. Although all expressions of PBL follow this basic structure, course goals, disciplinary content, and class size (along with other issues) may produce versions of PBL that appear very different from one another. Our own practices and experiences, as evidenced by the brief narratives that opened this chapter, are cases in point.

In our experience, the shift to PBL has made a noticeable difference in our students' ability to retain, integrate, and apply the knowledge they gained in the process of solving problems. We have also observed clear improvement in students' written and oral communications skills. The students who take our courses report a significant level of improvement in their understanding of course content and its professional and societal context, as well as a feeling of personal accomplishment at the end of the course.

## A Brief History

The modern PBL approach has its origins in reforms to medical education at McMaster University in Canada more than 40 years ago (Neufeld & Barrows, 1974), although the constructivist approach to education was advocated earlier by John Dewey and has its roots in ancient Greece. PBL curricula have since been implemented in more than 60 medical schools throughout the world, including Harvard University, the University of New Mexico, and the University of Sherbrooke (Albanese & Mitchell, 1993). PBL has since spread to postgraduate professional schools, including business, pharmacy, dentistry, optometry, and nursing (Delisle, 1997). At the college level, the most notable, widespread introduction of PBL in the curriculum has taken place at the University of Delaware (Duch, Groh, & Allen, 2001). A number of institutes have been developed for the training of faculty in the PBL process, including the Problem-

Based Learning Initiative at Southern Illinois University's School of Medicine and the Institute for Transforming Undergraduate Education at the University of Delaware.

PBL has been shown to promote a number of desirable characteristics in students, including 1) self-directed learning (Williams, 2001), 2) making substantive connections with course content that promote a deep level of processing and learning (Dominowski, 1998), and 3) collaborative learning (Allen & Rooney, 1998; Daiute & Dalton, 1993). In addition, the PBL approach has proven to be as effective as more conventional pedagogical methods with respect to learning outcomes (Albanese & Mitchell, 1993).

## What Isn't PBL

Like Libby, some of you may suspect you are already close to PBL, or perhaps think you may already be doing it. There are a number of teaching techniques that incorporate aspects of the PBL approach—group work, situational discussion, case studies—but it is important to distinguish these (often effective) approaches from "full blown" PBL. It may help us clarify the distinctiveness of the problem-based approach if we contrast it to some other common classroom practices.

### Problem Sets

Problem sets, whether at the end of textbook chapters or instructor-generated, are not the sorts of problems we are advocating. There are several differences. First, the nature of these problems is frequently such that there is only one correct solution, often found in the back of the book. In contrast, *effective PBL problems are more loosely structured.* There can be many different, equally valid solutions. Second, the paths leading to the correct solution to these problems are limited. Often there is only one way to arrive at the correct answer. In many instances, a cursory look at the examples found in the chapter or presented in a lecture puts students on the right track. There may be some unexpected twists and turns (e.g., unit conversions, the need to make a few simple assumptions), but once the right track is identified, it leads to the solution.

PBL problems, on the other hand, mimic authentic, complex problems in that *a path toward a reasonable solution usually isn't obvious.* Often, as in the real world, students may travel down a few blind alleys before they find their way to the strait and narrow path—which they may lose later on.

Finally, the problems traditionally given to students tend to be relatively simple, requiring that a few related skills or concepts be applied to get the correct answer. The purpose of such exercises is to develop the ability to apply those skills and concepts to a certain type of problem. In contrast, problems encountered in professional practice do not have clearly delineated boundaries; they take place in a complex context where even identifying the important issues can be a challenge. As such, they require that students first be able to determine the important questions before they pull together skills and concepts from different sources to develop a solution. PBL problems are designed to force students down the messy, iterative path of complexity and integration that is part of addressing real problems.

### Case Studies

As was true with problem sets, in case studies students are placed in highly structured situations that they are to discuss and consider. Cases are usually extensions of theories or principles established at the beginning of the unit, so groups of students most commonly read about a principle in the textbook and then discuss it in class with the professor before finally applying it to the case. *The order is inverted in a PBL classroom:* Students begin with the situation, and the theories and principles grow from grappling with how to address the problem.

### Immersion in a Topic

Many classes arrange the semester by themes or topics—read, research, and write a paper on X. In the most thoughtful of these course designs, students immerse themselves in a range of perspectives on and research about a compelling topic. Class sessions might engage students in discussion, small group work, and drafting multiple solutions to address the issue. Readings are usually offered from an anthology or course packet, and research strategies are generally well defined and presented during class sessions. In a PBL classroom, however, *the problem drives the research direction, as articulated by what students decide they need to learn in order to address the problem effectively.* Thus there are fewer boundaries and, as we'll see, less instructor control.

## Group Work

Group work is an integral part of the PBL process, but, as we saw in C.B.'s classroom, unless it is embedded in a problem-based context, it engages students less durably and often produces outcomes that are instructor driven rather than student initiated. In-class group work often involves asking students to get together to discuss an issue or develop a position after a short discussion. Such groups are usually ad hoc ("turn to your neighbor"), ephemeral, and are given a clear charge ("discuss this scene from the film *Lone Star* in light of Charles Taylor's account of the need for recognition and the politics of difference"). Such exercises certainly give students the opportunity to express and exchange ideas. And, if led properly, the ensuing discussions within and among groups can lead to new questions that will get students thinking about—and beyond—the original subject.

However, because of its ephemeral nature and the self-limiting tasks involved, most group work is structured in a manner that does not lead to an iterative group process. The new questions are generally not pursued further in additional group discussions. Rather, they are often simply dropped, or, at best, are left for individuals to pursue. As such, the opportunity for students to exchange, reflect on, and integrate new knowledge into the discussion is cut short. Groups in the PBL classroom are durable, providing the opportunity for continued discussion, reflection, and revision as students find new information and integrate it into a solution to the problem.

## Issues

Some of you, like José, might be thinking of a more radical shift, but realize that adopting PBL in your courses may be a daunting task. There certainly are challenges in making the switch to PBL. Whether you are going to try it in a limited manner in one of your courses, or you plan to give your courses an "extreme PBL makeover," you will find yourself confronting new and sometimes perplexing issues. We have run into many of those problems in our teaching over the years, and some have nearly led us to go back to our old ways of teaching. But we haven't.

The following are some issues we have encountered, both among ourselves and with our colleagues. Some are more difficult to deal with than others, but all are real, and all, we hope you'll come to see, can be overcome.

- *Class size.* "Sure, you can do this PBL thing if you teach a nice, small, upper-division seminar, but I teach Intro. Chemistry to 350 kids in a lecture hall the size of a gymnasium. How can I do this?"

- *Student resistance.* "Students don't like group work, especially the smart ones. They feel they are taken advantage of and don't learn anything from other students. And the slow ones just tune out."

- *Losing control.* "What do I do while all this discussion is going on? How will the students know that I am the professor? How do I know if they are learning anything?"

- *Problem preparation.* "How am I going to come up with real-life problems for my students? I teach Medieval history."

- *Lack of applicability.* "I teach art history at a community college. This PBL thing is for people in science—it really has nothing to offer my students."

- *Conservative colleagues.* "Everyone in my department lectures, and they expect junior faculty like me to follow suit."

- *Coverage.* "I don't cover nearly as much material when students do group work as when I lecture. And I must cover all the material in the syllabus in my nutrition course because my students need to pass a professional licensure exam to become registered dieticians."

- *Workload.* "It sounds like PBL is going to take a lot more preparation than lecturing. I am finally to the point where I can give my lectures in my sleep. Who has time to write all those complex problems, construct and grade challenging tests, and grade and comment on all those papers?"

- *Student evaluations.* "I need good student evaluations to get tenure. And students don't like to feel like they are being experimented on. I'm not going to risk poor evaluations by switching to PBL."

The following chapters address these and many of the other issues involved in using PBL. Some are unique to PBL, and, of course, others are issues regardless of the teaching technique involved.

# 2
# Changing the Landscape

Tinkering with course design is part and parcel of the academic enterprise. Many of us continually reimagine our courses, wondering if a new example there, a more contemporary illustration here, or less lecture on this and more discussion on that would encourage deeper learning in our students and make our class time more engaging and productive. For the most part, however, our redesigned courses resemble their predecessors: We make presentations, we place students in groups to discuss or debate ideas, and we assign students papers, projects, and exams to assess just how it all worked. Our courses may be fresh, and we may be refreshed, but our approach to course design remains traditional.

There is, of course, nothing wrong with such tinkering; indeed, much of it goes well beyond minor adjustments in assignments, lectures, and pacing, to more substantial changes in what we plan to accomplish in a course and how those new goals will demand changes in how we conduct both the in-class and out-of-class portions of our courses. Still, most of our efforts leave us in the position we have always been in—the choreographer of an elaborate performance where each step is thought through, mentally rehearsed, so that at the end of every day we know what will come next.

When we adapt our courses to PBL, things are different because PBL is not the tinkering we are used to. Rather, it is a dramatic change in how our instruction is conceived, how the content of our courses is approached, and how our roles as faculty members are enacted. So, before we decide that PBL is for us (and our students) we want to do a bit of thinking about what is going to change in our classrooms, and what we need to do to get ready for how different things will be.

## Changing Ourselves

PBL injects significant changes into the roles we play in the classroom. Ordinarily, we are both in charge and in control, the focus of attention. When we speak, students pay attention (or at least we hope they do), even if we are only posing questions or merely summarizing the reporting that has gone on in small group activity. Our class time moves on a schedule we set, perhaps speeding up or slowing down depending on our assessment of how well students have mastered the material at hand.

If we think back to our voices in Chapter 1, each of them contains at least a tacit acknowledgement of the anchoring role we played in the classroom conduct of our courses: José's metaphor about the different directional notions of passenger and driver, Libby's sense that the situations in her writing courses were not quite provocative enough, and C.B.'s admission that after a few minutes of student discussion, he often ended up solving the problems he had posed. In one way or another each of us was (or could, when we chose, become) the main attraction, the one with all the answers.

### Shifting the Center

PBL shifts the center of our courses from what we do and what we say to the problem with which our students are confronted. More than that, however, PBL transforms our roles from the purveyors of knowledge to participants in a process, from the masters of problems to managers of groups. This shift is more than the already overused "sage on the stage to guide on the side" phrase implies. PBL does not merely move us from the center to the margins of otherwise ordinary classroom activity. It also shifts the control, pacing, and direction of classroom activity to those engaged actively in the problem—our students.

C.B.:

*One of the more interesting thoughts I have during the PBL portions of my course is the idea that I could leave the room and nothing would change, and no one would notice. I wouldn't actually do it, but to see and hear hundreds of students in small groups working away on a problem makes you wonder if you have any role other than timekeeper. Of course, you also get to listen in on conversations, but that can create more temptation than you are able to bear. When students have headed down a blind alley in the pursuit of a solution—and they often do—you want to help them, to say, "Wait, why not try this instead?" rather than just listen and learn what comes next. I have to remind myself of why we're doing this in the first place, and why it's important that they find the way back and the way out, without my often too helpful intervention.*

Libby:

*The pacing of my classes had always followed a predictable and generally effective pattern: first, workshops on the homework, then a short lecture on a new concept for today, followed by all-class discussion on that new concept, ending with individualized practice in preparation for the homework. The next class, same pattern. All in all, it was a pretty good structure for using in-class time effectively. Switching to PBL, however, meant cutting the short lecture and discussion and presenting students with the next phase of the problem to let them figure out how to proceed. I quickly found this caused me to listen differently. Instead of listening to see how well they were understanding and applying the concepts I had just presented to them, I needed to pay attention to their processes and tools, learning about the resources students already had at their disposal. Thus began my new-found respect for cell phones and instant messaging.*

José:

*I purposely listen to students' conversations because I want to know what direction they are heading in with their solution and whether they are getting it. In a sense it's like listening to what's going on in their minds— something I wondered about frequently when I lectured. I've found that the answer is often more encouraging than I anticipated. Students have a lot of interesting— if sometimes misguided and off-topic—ideas to offer.*

Hung, Bailey, and Jonassen (2003) describe this transformation of our classroom roles by setting the "traditional professor" in opposition to the "tutor" implicit in the practice of PBL. Although an instructionally skilled "professor" may not be as opposed to a PBL "tutor" as their continuum implies, Hung et al. are correct in their sense that PBL can put us in unfamiliar and often uncomfortable situations.

For us, that discomfort was minimized by our commitment to engaging students actively. Well before we determined to convert them to PBL, each of our courses involved activities in which student participation and collaboration were given at least a loose rein. Case studies, small group discussions, and role playing are not quite the same as PBL, but they did give us practice in standing aside to allow what students were doing to become the focus of a class session or two or three.

There is probably a lesson in that. Courses do not need to— and probably should not—be converted to PBL directly from a highly traditional lecture–text–notes–exams format. This is especially true in large courses, where both we and our students have come to expect rather conventional instructor-directed teaching. Without at least some sense of what we are getting into—say, managing 30 groups in an auditorium, or answering mundane but urgent–to–students questions like, "If my group doesn't work well, am I going to be penalized?"—the promise of PBL can easily be lost. For students, too, a sudden shift to PBL from the more passive (no matter how engaged) role as note-taker can be disconcerting unless they have had some classroom experiences that bridge the gap (see Woods, 1996, for a discussion).

## Honing Our Skills

The transformation can be (and probably should be) made in stages, over a couple of semesters, as course design incorporates first some group activities, then more, giving us a chance to see how it will work and to hone the skills necessary to be effective as participants (rather than purveyors) and managers (rather than masters). It takes both time and practice to learn how best to help students navigate a problem. Letting go of the idea that we'll let them work for a bit and then ride to their rescue does not mean that we now (as tutors, not professors) stand by idly watching group after group flounder until they (and probably we) give up on PBL.

Hung, Bailey, and Jonassen (2003) provide a particularly useful summary of the PBL literature devoted to those "tutoring" skills that strike a balance between the unstructured nature of the problems and the support and encouragement that students—particularly those early in their college careers—need as they seek solutions. They argue that successful instruction in PBL settings demands that we develop skills along three dimensions. First, we need to be able to communicate with our students in a way that is "cognitively congruent" with their own intellectual processes. Of course, the capacity to use language, concepts, and examples that are familiar to our students is part of any form of effective instruction, but in PBL its importance is brought into sharp relief. Often students do not know where or how to begin to attack a problem, and so even before they begin they seem stymied. A simple question or comment can make students see the problem as less alien and more tractable than they first thought.

Libby:

> *I've used a problem to begin my first-year writing course that places students in teams for a writing-intensive internship of the sort they might actually do later in their college careers. I tell them only that they are working for the local Congressman whose district includes the university. To prepare for the first day of work, I ask them to find out everything they can about him: his stances, his votes, his appearances, and so on. Some groups, of course, know who he is and get started right away; others share a collective shake of the head and look despondent, saying, "We've never heard of him, so we're kind of stuck." I could give them a few hints about his party affiliation or other aspects that put him in the news regularly, but that's what I want them to find out. So instead I pose a simple question: "Ever Google anybody?"*

Second, we need to develop our skills at modeling appropriate problem-solving behavior without actually solving the problem at hand. To put it in educationese, we need to model the metacognitive processes (Hung, Bailey, & Jonassen, 2003) involved in the tasks assigned to students. In essence, we need to be able to show students how to "solve the problem of solving the problem." Our ability to articulate that process, without at the same time solving the problem, can go a long way toward giving students a framework that will support the deep learning that PBL is meant to foster.

José:

> *Students' first attempt at solving a problem often involves trying very hard to get answers from me. And, when I first started using PBL in my courses, I had to fight the knee-jerk response to give them answers, to show them the way. My strategy is to answer their questions with another question: What do you think? This prompts them to articulate their thoughts and, in*

*the process, frequently either figure out the answer to the question or decide on a path to find out what the answer may be on their own. Only when I have observed them struggle for a long time—and often in the interest of time—do I answer their questions with questions that suggest reasonable avenues to pursue.*

In addition to our capacity to meet students where they are and our ability to model "solving the problem of solving the problem"— skills that reflect our role as participants in the process—we also need some facility along a third dimension: managing the process of group work both within and among the various groups in our classrooms. PBL is absolutely dependent on effective group work, and our ability to encourage productive discussion, provide useful feedback, and support meaningful integration is crucial if our students are to make the most of their PBL experiences (Hung, Bailey, & Jonassen, 2003).

C.B.:

*I spend most of my time during PBL units trying to make sure the groups are working, both in the simple sense of determining if they are actually at work on the problem as well as the more sophisticated sense of determining their productivity and involvement and if they are working toward a solution in a coherent and holistic way. If you watch a group at work, even if only briefly, you can tell a lot. You can see who is a participant and who has been shut out, so you might have to make space for the silent (or the silenced): "So, José, what do you think about that idea of privacy as central to human rights?" You can tell when things have been misunderstood: "Libby, would Ignatieff agree that cultural rights should take precedence over individual rights?" You can also get a sense of when any number of groups might benefit from similar feedback: "A lot of you have this, and a lot of you have that, and some of you have this. Is there a way to put these parts together?"*

There is nothing magical about any of these skills. All of them really are integral to good teaching. Nevertheless, when we begin to think about PBL, we should be sure that these skills are part of our repertoire.

## Changing Our Courses

Once we have decided we're ready to go ahead with PBL, we can turn our attention to the restructuring and reorganization of our course plans and classroom activities. This part of the process can seem deceptively simple. We just need to fashion or find an engaging, complex problem, introduce it to the class, organize our students into groups, and then set them loose while we remind ourselves of our transformed roles. Voilá! Problem-based learning up and running!

Our voices in Chapter 1 could certainly create the impression that once our decisions for PBL were made and our problems identified, each of us merely set the process in motion without giving much, if any, thought to how it would all turn out. Although there may be some attraction in that sort of academic derring-do, it is not really how things happened for us, and it is not the way traditional lecture and discussion courses are refashioned into PBL offerings. We did a good deal more planning than that. The issues we confronted make a useful checklist of things to think about and decide on before launching PBL in our courses.

### Extent and Duration of PBL

The power of PBL to transform passive classrooms into active centers of engaged learning has led some of its advocates to present it as an all or nothing choice. PBL works (or at least works best), they say, when courses are turned inside out in their entirety: problems replace lectures, learning teams replace isolated students, tutors replace professors, all PBL, all the time (Duch, Groh, & Allen, 2001). There is certainly merit in this position. PBL is robust, and it can be used profitably from the first class of the semester until the last.

José:

> *I teach four different undergraduate courses—all in soil science—using "full-on PBL": all PBL, all the time. I decided to do this primarily because the students that take my courses will be applying the content and skills they learn in a problem-solving setting once they graduate, whether they work as consultants, regulators, technicians, or researchers. Their work will require that they collaborate with professionals from different walks of life, that they integrate knowledge from a wide variety of sources, and, perhaps most importantly, that they will have to solve messy, open-ended, poorly structured problems with real consequences. PBL works well as a training vehicle for future environmental problem solvers.*

There are, however, ways to think about PBL that do not commit us to an all-or-nothing approach, and there are some good reasons to at least consider using it in a less expansive manner. First, like any other instructional technique, PBL creates a certain routine and rhythm over the course of a semester. Students work in groups, find out what they know about the problem, decide what they need to know next, conduct some research, and return to their groups to begin the process again. This cycle (Duch, Groh, & Allen, 2001), no matter how imaginative the problems, can—if other activities are not interspersed—create a humdrum sense of "here we go again."

Libby:

> *For writing-rich humanities classes like first-year writing, full-on PBL may not make a lot of sense. For one thing, students need to write individual projects for individual grades, although it is certainly fine for those projects to have been shaped through interaction and collaboration with others. On the other hand, one substantial PBL problem seemed the perfect way to establish most of my instructional goals: collaborative*

*learning, constant deep revision, critical research, a wide range of genres and audiences and reasons for writing, and an awareness that writing can have real social consequences.*

Second, with its profound commitment to group work, PBL tends to create environments that advantage students with particular learning styles and skills. This is, of course, true of any instructional strategy, but if PBL is the only way students can engage in our courses, we may inadvertently but systematically isolate or marginalize some students who could be profitably engaged if we used some combination of classroom strategies (see Erickson, Peters, & Strommer, 2006, for a discussion of learning styles and instructional strategies).

Third, PBL is better suited for the achievement of some student outcomes than it is for others. To be sure, the outcomes that PBL supports and sustains—critical thinking and analysis, effective communications skills, development of lifelong learning skills, among others—are profoundly important for higher education (Duch, Groh, & Allen, 2001), but they are not the only legitimate goals for our courses. Sometimes, particularly in those courses that begin disciplinary sequences or constitute parts of some general education programs, it is good for us to be purveyors of knowledge, and while PBL does not preclude students' acquisition of basic facts and theoretical frameworks, it is probably not the most efficient or effective way to produce those outcomes.

C.B.:

*One of the reasons I was attracted to PBL—in addition to its promise of deep learning—was how different the PBL classroom I envisioned would be from the way things usually went. Even though my course was a pretty active version of a 500-student lecture, there was a certain pattern—I'd talk, they'd talk or they'd talk, I'd talk—that by the end of October had become pretty predictable. The idea of breaking that routine by turning a portion of the course inside out was really quite alluring. PBL seemed to offer a structured way to get them to do the work of the course while seeming fun, manageable, and different.*

*I wasn't willing to give up everything I'd developed over the years for a couple of reasons. As I mentioned earlier, the course was working. Students liked it and they reported that they learned a lot. But, more than that, I had been very intentional about developing different activities, different approaches, and different examples in an effort to create at least something in the course that each student felt a special affinity toward. To throw all that over and go completely to PBL just didn't seem sensible to me.*

*It seemed possible to add PBL to the repertoire without subtracting other things that were working. Thinking about it as a short, contained bit of the course to be shuffled in with other short, contained bits seemed to be the answer.*

So how do you decide whether to go all the way with PBL or to integrate it, a bit here, a bit there, with other instructional strategies? That is hard to say for sure, but there are some considerations.

## Class Size

Although effective instruction in all courses depends on variety, this becomes especially true as enrollments increase. In smaller classes, there are ways we can attend to students' learning styles and skills that are independent of how the course is conducted. As numbers increase, our capacities in that regard are quickly overwhelmed, and we need to vary our instructional strategies if we are to provide comfortable learning environments for all of our students. If you have small classes, think about all PBL, all the time. If you have large classes, think about a PBL unit or two to mix in with other forms of effective instruction.

*SYNTHESIS ALSO*

## Instructional Goals

PBL is particularly well suited for those courses whose main thrust is to help students develop the capacity for critical thinking and analysis. If your course is focused primarily on those outcomes— say, an upper-division course for majors, or a general education course where methods of inquiry and modes of analysis are more important than acquisition of knowledge—think about all PBL, all the time. If you have a course whose expressed outcomes are more varied, think about a PBL unit or two to mix in with other forms of effective instruction.

## Problem Library

A good problem is the heart and soul of PBL; a collection of good problems is absolutely essential if PBL is going to support student learning and sustain student attention throughout a semester. If you have a collection of good problems that are based on real-world situations, embed content objectives, and require higher-order critical thinking and analysis, think about all PBL, all the time. If you have only one or two good problems, think about a PBL unit or two to mix in with other forms of effective instruction.

## Complexity and Sequencing of Problems

It is not surprising that PBL is called what it is: The learning that occurs is indeed dependent on the problem that initiates it. The more complex and less structured the problem, the deeper and richer the learning that is waiting in the process that produces a solution. That is the good news. The bad news is that the more complex and less structured the problem, the more daunting and difficult the PBL learning environment. Choosing problems at an appropriate level of complexity and, if you are going to be using multiple problems during a course, finding an appropriate sequence (easy to hard, easy and hard alternating, etc.) are critically important decisions in planning a PBL unit or course.

Libby:

> *I start my courses with a challenging problem to destabilize students' sense of what a writing class will be like (essays, essays, and more essays) and to establish good inquiry habits that will serve them well regardless of the direction they choose. Even though many of my first-semester students are nervous about their first college class, the pacing of my problems allows for enough support within the class and a sense of accomplishment at having nailed something pretty complex within the first three weeks of college. They may have expected to write about "my most memorable relationship," and instead they compose fact sheets and FAQs and web sites and white papers. I like to think their later essays will be more sophisticated and daring if they begin the course with a meaty, unstructured problem.*

There are circumstances, however, when less complex or perhaps more structured problems are appropriate.

C.B.:

> *The problems I've introduced are probably complex—I developed one around the issue of reparations for slavery, for instance—but because I have a large class of primarily first-year students, and because I want to devote only some parts of my course to PBL, I try to structure them more than is probably typical of PBL in advanced courses. Sometimes I've indicated what the first step in the process is, sometimes I've suggested taking a particular perspective, other times I've supplied some evidence to help move them forward in a problem. This may not be PBL in its "pure" form, but given the constraints of time and experience, I think students still get a sense of the process and most of the benefits of PBL.*

Our decisions on the sorts of problems we chose to introduce revolved around three issues:

- *Extent of PBL use.* The more PBL, the more we can think about introducing increasingly complex and unstructured problems.

- *Course level and focus.* The higher the level and the tighter the focus, the more we can think about introducing increasingly complex and unstructured problems.

- *Expected outcomes.* The more advanced the outcomes, the more we can think about introducing increasingly complex and unstructured problems.

## Forming Groups

We do not often think about the process of forming students into groups for discussions, case studies, and the like. Generally, we say something like, "Make some small groups," and leave it to them to sort it out reasonably. We might intervene occasionally, to break up groups that have grown too large, or to try to rebalance groups along gender, race, or other lines. This casual approach is generally effective largely because most of the groups our students form are transitory; they come into existence only for a short task and dissolve when that task is completed. If they turn out to be dysfunctional, well, we can try again next time.

Things are very different in PBL. Groups are durable; once formed, they stay together over time, for several weeks or even an entire semester. When PBL groups work well, their durability is a good thing. When they do not, there is no getting away from them, either for us or, more importantly, for our students who are mired in them. The strategy we use to form PBL groups is a high-stakes game, and thinking the process through before we begin can help ensure that each group will create a productive learning environment.

In general, there are two approaches to group formation to consider before launching PBL. The first—self-selection—is the one most of us are familiar with already. Students choose their group mates based on their own preferences. Not surprisingly, this approach is one most students like; after all, they get to be with their friends, their roommates, or acquaintances from others settings. Because students (at least most of them) feel comfortable in self-selected groups, this strategy is worth thinking about when we consider moving to PBL. For most students, a PBL classroom is an alien environment (at least initially), and a "group of their own" may help them navigate it.

There are, of course, some logistical reasons for using self-selected PBL groups. Large classes, even courses with moderately sized enrollments, can make more intentional methods of group creation unworkable. Even when that is the case, we should probably be more attentive to their selections than usual. We need to remember there is a lot at stake here. The PBL groups students select are made in a day, but they cannot be unmade so easily.

C.B.:

> *I don't have any way of assigning students to groups except to let them choose their partners. But I don't have to let their PBL groups be the first groups they've formed in the course, and I don't have to assume once they've formed there is nothing I can do to try to address things that don't seem likely to be productive.*
>
> *One of the more important things is, I think, to give students some idea of group work before we move into our first PBL unit. We usually begin PBL in about the fourth week of the semester, so I make it a point to have several group activities, some in groups of four or five, some in groups of three, and some in pairs. That way, students have the opportunity to find more potential partners than they might otherwise. By the time they sign up for their PBL group, they've had the opportunity to get a taste of working with a number of different students. I hope this helps them make more informed*

> *choices about who they'd like to work with over a two-week period.*
>
> *Another thing I've done is to provide some guidance for their choices. I distribute a set of instructions about PBL and forming groups, and on it, I encourage them to be inclusive, to try to make groups that contain both men and women, to ask people they know and people they'd like to know, and so on. Most students are sympathetic to the idea of inclusion, so I think this reminder helps create groups balanced along lines of difference.*
>
> *I also try to circulate throughout the room just after the PBL groups have formed and are ready to be introduced to the problem, so I can see what the groups look like. Sometimes, I'll try to make some adjustments if they seem natural and relatively easily accomplished. My groups are supposed to contain three to five members. So, for instance, if I see three men as a group and a nearby group of three women, I may suggest they combine, even though the result is a group a bit bigger than I want.*

In spite of our comfort (and theirs) with self-selected groups, it is probably better educational practice to assign students to groups with an eye toward both the task embedded in the problem and the issues of difference among the students in our classroom. In small classes, we can be quite intentional in this regard, choosing students' group assignments along several criteria simultaneously.

Libby:

> *When I begin a problem on the first day of class—really, in the first five minutes of class—I can't assign groups based on any knowledge of their strengths, weaknesses, backgrounds, or values. So I take my chances with the alphabetical roster, and watch for issues in the group*

*dynamics. With PBL as only the first portion of that class, I don't need to worry as much about group longevity. Having said that, I'm envious of a colleague who was able to control enrollment in his class such that he could devise five perfectly balanced groups. Each contained one political or social scientist, one biologist or life scientist, and one student in the humanities, either in languages or philosophy. Thus each member of each team brought to the table different expertise, different approaches, and different perspectives, all of which were equally valuable to the project.*

There are other methods of group assignment we can employ. Random assignment, counting off, and so on can avoid some of the pitfalls of self-selection (cliques, isolated students), but they do not assure balanced groups, and they do not take advantage of what we might know about students (their majors, their previous course work) that may be relevant to the PBL process.

José:

*I thought about trying to assign students to groups. You know, some good ones, some not so good ones, so that the groups would all start out on even footing. But I decided against it, mostly because I frequently don't know a student's strengths and weaknesses before they enroll in my course. This is particularly true for my introductory soil science course, since I meet the students for the first time when they show up on the first day of class. So, rather than attempting to engineer groups, I assign them randomly on the first day of class. They remain in that group from that day forward until the end of the semester.*

Effective groups are essential to the success of PBL, and that effectiveness is often ensured (or undermined) at the outset, when groups are formed. We cannot, of course, guarantee that every group will function effectively, but devoting some attention to the dynamics of group formation can help.

- *Group size.* We (and others) think small is better, even though that means more groups who need our management and modeling. A group of four seems to be ideal, but three or five will work as well. More than five is not advisable, except perhaps to address issues of group composition or to integrate a lone or isolated student.

- *Selection process.* If we can assign students to PBL groups in some intentional way, we probably should. But because intentional assignment works best in small classes, it is not often possible when our enrollments begin to expand. If we allow students to self-select groups, we should try to shape those choices in ways that encourage inclusion through both classroom practice and verbal instruction.

- *Group composition.* Whatever selection process we settle on, we should be attentive to the mix of students in our PBL groups. Reminders to students about the importance of inclusion as groups are formed, and perhaps some gentle intervention to prevent or correct imbalances are some ways to ensure successfully composed groups.

## Assessment and Grading

Making decisions about how we are going to evaluate students is an important part of any course planning process, but it takes on special significance when we are thinking about introducing PBL. The vast majority of our student assessment practices, whether our classrooms involve group activities or not, are designed to measure what individual students know and are able to do at the end of a unit or the end of a course. Because group work is woven into the very fabric of problem-based learning, the individual focus on our usual assessment practices—exams, papers, reviews—needs to be rethought, and probably revised.

Although we'll devote a good deal more attention to this issue in Chapter 5, there are some issues to consider as we plan our courses for PBL. The cooperative group work (and learning) that lies at the heart of PBL requires that our assessment practices take into account two separate but related features. First, we need to plan to assess the work of the group as a whole. By its very nature, PBL puts students in circumstances where they cannot succeed unless the other members of their group succeed as well. This "positive interdependence" is a central aspect of the learning PBL induces, and we need to develop some valid and reliable means to assess it.

Second, we need to develop assessment techniques that hold individual students accountable. Group work always carries with it the risk of free-riders, students who are passive or who participate only minimally, relying on others to complete the assignments and earn them their grade. When group work is fleeting or a limited part of students' grades, such free-riding may be annoying, but it is generally easily managed. In a PBL course, free-riders are a serious threat to the learning process. Our exhortation to students to become actively engaged in PBL may reduce the number of free-riders, but by itself it probably will not eliminate them. Assessment processes that hold individuals accountable for their participation, contribution, and learning are more effective.

José:

*I do my best to "mix it up" when it comes to assessment: roughly equal parts of group and individual responsibilities. This does a couple of things. It makes it clear to the students that both types of activities are valued. It also allows the students (and me) to get a better sense of what they can accomplish when they join forces to solve a problem, and it provides an indication of what the individuals have managed to learn from the process. Students skeptical of PBL are often pleasantly surprised by their performance in individual assessments, much to their astonishment.*

This is a delicate balance. We do not want to focus our assessment so intently on group products that individual students can, if they choose, duck their responsibilities and hide from the consequences. At the same time, we do not want to undermine the positive cooperative work of the group through assessment practices that minimize the collective performance by paying attention only to what individuals know or are able to do.

In addition to the group-individual balance in our assessment practices, we also need to consider how often to assess students in a PBL format. Because PBL seems to have a logical and pedagogically appropriate endpoint—when the problem is solved—we are often tempted to delay introducing assessment until students have reached that stage. This may work effectively for PBL courses for upper-division students, but for first-year students or novice practitioners of a discipline, postponing the feedback that assessment provides is probably not a good idea.

C.B.:

> My first PBL unit creates some anxiety in my students. They like working in groups and they're excited about the issues in the problem, but they want to know how they are doing, if they're getting it. I do give them some verbal assurance—"That seems to be a good start. Where are you going next?"—that sort of thing. But I also collect products from each group at each step of the problem. I give this a relatively quick "credit or no credit" assessment and then select some to show to the class in our next session. Although seeing what other groups have done may compromise the "purity" of PBL, I think the feedback that comes from seeing good work (along with the credit or no credit grade) allays their fears and gives them enough guidance to keep going without giving away the game.

Again, we want to strike a balance. We do not necessarily want to grade each step in the problem-solving process; after all, part of the power of PBL is learning that on the way to a solution, wrong turns are often taken, discovered, and corrected. But we also do not want to leave students wondering how they are doing and whether what they are producing is good enough to earn them the grades they desire.

As we plan the introduction of PBL in our courses, then, we need to reflect on how we are going to assess our students, the products they produce, and the learning they demonstrate. There's much more in Chapter 5, but these are the considerations to develop a sound assessment plan in our PBL courses.

- *Assess the work of groups.* This is perhaps the easiest aspect of getting ready to do PBL. We can treat group products as if they were individual products, and assign grades to them and the participant individuals accordingly.

- *Assess the work of individuals as group and individual learners.* This is a more difficult challenge. Disentangling a student's contributions and learning from group products can be daunting, raising—as it does—issues of fairness and reliability. However, unless we do this, we may leave our students and ourselves open to a serious free-rider problem.

- *Frequency of assessment.* We may choose to assess students only at the end of a problem-based unit, but if our students are younger or less experienced, we will probably want to assess them periodically as they work their way through a problem.

## Changing Our Students

Nearly every discussion of PBL (including this one) begins with the necessary transformation in how we as faculty see and enact our roles. That is as it should be. Faculty behavior sets the tone for classroom environments, and unless we manage ourselves in ways that are conducive to PBL, we will not see the kinds of learning that drew us to it in the first place. Changes in faculty behavior are, however, not sufficient to ensure the success of PBL. Our students need to make some changes as well. These changes may not be as dramatic as those involved in abandoning the orderly sureness of the lecture for the messy uncertainty of PBL, but they are real and they do demand some of our attention.

Most students at colleges and universities are, at least to some degree, used to the practices of active learning. They have probably done group projects, participated in discussions, worked on case studies, and the like in both secondary school and in other courses on our campuses. But, because PBL turns the learning process inside out—with the problems coming first and instruction emerging as students work toward a solution—and because it focuses on extended cooperative group work—with students themselves substantially affecting the pacing and direction of the course—students may find themselves in a classroom environment that is a bit more active than they are used to.

Libby:

> *Students have come to expect a fairly standard first day of class: Professor enters the classroom, reads through the roster trying dutifully to record pronunciations and preferred nicknames, then walks through the policies and the syllabus, while students try their best to listen attentively despite the deadliness of droning through a bunch of policies.*
>
> *So when I start the first minutes of the very first class with a problem—I don't yet know their names, they don't yet know mine—most students are puzzled by the break in the routine. Some are pleased, some are disconcerted, most are willing to dive in and get engaged right away. Once they break into groups they learn each other's names. After they report out their findings—about two-thirds of the way into class—I learn their names and make sure they know mine. It's important that they know mundane things before I do,*

*as it subtly seems to move the center of expertise from me
to them. They rather like knowing stuff before I do.*

We can help ease our students' transitions from the active learning of a more typical classroom to the full immersion of the PBL classroom by carefully explaining why we have chosen this method of instruction. Our own stories, much like those in Chapter 1, may help students understand our thinking about the course and their learning, and it may help them develop a willingness to tolerate a bit more ambiguity than they would otherwise. We should also be clear about just what PBL involves, for us and for them. The syllabus is the best place to do this, and the first class is the best time to direct their attention to how different PBL might seem from their other academic experiences.

José:

*My syllabus spells out up front the objectives of the course, how PBL works, and how they will be assessed, as groups and as individuals. This includes papers, presentations, and exams, as well as peer evaluations. Once I've gone over the syllabus, I assign students to groups randomly, inform them that they are stuck with each other for the rest of the semester, and give them the first problem. As they go through the initial PBL cycle, you can almost hear the gears turning: Group papers? Exams? No lectures? How am I going to learn anything? Is this guy for real? In time they find out that I am.*

We also should be careful about assuming too much about our students' experiences with active learning. Students may well have worked in groups, but they are less likely to have had so much riding on productive group work as is necessarily the case in a PBL setting. There is some dispute about the wisdom of having students spend time working through issues of group dynamics, but because of the centrality of effective group work to PBL, some attention should be devoted to these issues.

*use the first class*
*create problem*
*They have to learn*
*about each other*

One potentially useful idea is to have students approach the PBL group work through a problem involving an imaginary group that is having trouble working together. The task can be straightforward and resolvable in a class period or two. "What are the issues that have emerged in the dysfunctional group, and what procedures would you recommend to resolve those issues—and to keep them from recurring?" As students work through the problem, they accomplish two things simultaneously: They get some practice at working together to solve a problem, and they develop some self-generated guidelines for productive group work. This practice problem and the resulting guidelines may pay dividends down the road. This approach is discussed further in Chapter 5.

Thinking about what students need to do differently for PBL to succeed is especially important if the course is large. Large courses invite students to imagine themselves in the relatively passive role of listener and note-taker, not as an active and engaged member of a problem-solving group. We should try to remind students early on—and the first day is not too soon—that in spite of what they expect of this large class (or what they have experienced in the past), things are going to be different in ways that will both engage them and challenge them.

C.B.:

> *I spend as much of the first class as I can having students talk to each other. And I continue that over the next several days as well. What they talk about is simpler and more accessible than the problem I'll present them with, but the practice they get at being active is important. There is always a temptation to want to tell them a few things, to lecture for a few sessions before they get started, but I think that just assures them that no matter what I say about PBL or active learning, things really aren't going to be different. Getting them talking right away makes them believe that I mean what I say and it sets the right tone for introducing the PBL unit in a week or two.*

To get our students ready for PBL, we should make a concerted effort to articulate our own convictions about teaching and learning and to engage our classes early on in the practices we say we are committed to. Some ways to do this include the following:

- *Be direct.* Explain to students why we have chosen PBL as a teaching strategy. This will help them (and us) understand what we expect of them and why we expect it.

- *Ensure familiarity with group work.* It is important that students are aware of the practices necessary for successful cooperative learning, especially over time. We should think about some preliminary activities for students that will help them hone the skills and sense of responsibility necessary for good group work and successful engagement with PBL.

- *Consider class size.* In small classes, our students probably expect to be actively involved and so will find a change to PBL less dramatic. In large classes, we need to be careful not to let passive expectations set in by getting students involved early on and in advance of our introduction to PBL.

Preparing ourselves, our courses, and our students for a very different learning environment are important first steps in the process of transforming traditional courses and classrooms to PBL. Many aspects of this process are similar to the sort of thinking we do about any course before we actually undertake instruction. As we have seen, however, PBL casts a very different light on some aspects of course design.

None of our PBL planning will produce the results we desire if the problems do not challenge students to engage in the process of learning. PBL begins with good problems. There are no halfway measures, no shortcuts. Writing problems is hard work, but it is also fun and rewarding. We turn our attention to that task now.

# 3

# No Problems? No Problem

Our first challenge in developing successful PBL courses or units lies in designing the right problem. Where to start? What should be included? How much information is too much? Too little? Will it catch their interest? We knew that warnings, admonishments, and anecdotes about flawed and unsuccessful problems were scattered throughout the PBL literature, so each of us approached writing our first problem with visions of classroom disaster lurking in the backs of our minds. The first problems we produced were not perfect—far from it—but they did not produce the chaos we feared either.

We may have had beginners' luck, but as we have refined those initial problems and produced new ones, we have discovered that successful PBL problems—those that produce rich discussion and deep learning—tend to be developed along similar lines and share a set of characteristics in terms of structure and presentation. Keeping these things in mind as we sit down to write problems will not guarantee success, but it will raise the odds that all of us (even those just starting out) can implement PBL with a solid problem, rich in the possibility for significant student learning.

## The Basics

The best way to begin thinking about the characteristics of good PBL problems is to take a close look at one that has been used successfully. "Fecal Follies" (Appendix 3.1) is a problem José has used in a senior-level soil microbiology course where PBL is the exclusive method of instruction. Fecal Follies illustrates the basic organization of PBL prompts: a title (in this case, a whimsical one), an introduction that sets the stage for the problem, a section that outlines the specifics of

43

the problem, and open-ended questions to get students started moving toward a solution.

The narrative in the introduction creates a real-world setting for the problem posed. The main character (the student) is going back to work for her former employer, an environmental microbiology consulting firm, Tiny Solutions, that is focusing its attention on the rejuvenation of failed septic systems. The initial aspects of the problem and associated questions involve a time-honored conundrum faced by environmental scientists—what, where, how, and when to sample, given limited resources. These issues, of course, could be covered through lectures and presentations, but instead they are embedded in a PBL setting so that students will delve deeper into the complexities of sampling environmental matrices.

Fecal Follies does not provide much information that students can use to fashion a solution. Because this problem is designed for advanced students, the spare structure of the problem is probably appropriate; they have enough experience and background knowledge to be able to navigate the unstructured nature of the situation. There are, however, times when we have provided students with additional information in order to jumpstart them toward a solution or to make a difficult and complex problem more manageable.

José:

> *When I started using PBL in my courses, I provided students only with the bare-bones problem. In time I realized that inclusion of additional information could help my students work through PBL problems more effectively. Now my problems often include a limited list of resources (e.g., articles, web sites, textbook chapters) to help them get started. I also provide a timetable for all activities related to the problem, which sets expectations for time management. The information helps allay the anxiety generated by open-ended problems, particularly in first- and second-year students.*

Our decisions about how much (or how little) information to provide to students are driven by the level of our courses and the complexity of the problems we have created. In general, the lower the level of the course and more complex the problem, the more information or structured phases we have provided. The additional information does not contain a solution to the problem, but it does provide a readily accessible background that can stimulate students' thinking about the issues in the problem without their having to track down the basic facts of the matter at hand.

C.B.:

> *The first problem I developed for my introductory sociology class revolved around the controversy over reparations for slavery. As I began writing the problem it seemed to me that students could sink their teeth into it only if they knew something about the history of reparations proposals and the dimensions of the contemporary dispute. Finding those things out could, of course, have been the first part of the problem, but I wanted them to deal with the controversy right off the bat, so instead of asking them to find the information they needed, I gave it to them.*

"Reparations for Slavery: Paying the Piper?" a problem from C.B.'s large introductory sociology course (Appendix 3.2), provides an illustration of how a background discussion and supporting information can help students get started on a problem they may not know much about. The problem itself is straightforward—advise the university president on the proper stance of the institution with regard to reparations. But without the background and references distributed with the problem (see the bulleted paragraphs), thinking about the importance and complexity of the issue might become secondary to the students' efforts to sort out just what the reparations issue was all about.

Sometimes, however, we want our students to do the basic investigative work to discover the nature and dimensions of the issue we want them to deal with. For instance, in Libby's writing course, she expects students to develop the ability to discover, assess, and process information available from a variety of sources. Her PBL problem (Appendix 3.3) begins with this task and proceeds from the information-gathering stage to the other aspects of the problem.

Libby:

> *I want my students to know how to get and evaluate information that they can use as the foundation for their writing. So it seemed natural to ask them to begin with only the knowledge they bring with them. It takes some time away from the writing projects that are part of the problem, but it is more important to get them looking beyond their own knowledge right away.*

Each of the examples we have introduced differs in the complexity of the problem they pose, how much information they provide, and the nature of the initial tasks they ask students to perform. In spite of those differences, however, each of our problems immerses students in a situation where they have to think about what they already know and what they need to find out in order to solve the problems we have constructed. That is PBL.

## Sources for Problems

Most faculty are already familiar with a variety of materials that can be transformed into a PBL problem suitable to the needs of their courses. We have taken particular problems, or the inspiration to write problems, from a wide array of sources. Some are especially fruitful.

- Problems at the ends of chapters in undergraduate textbooks, commonly found in science, mathematics, and economics texts

- Problem sets, case studies, and exam questions that we have written for our courses

- Our own professional practice, research, or consulting projects

- Research and scholarly articles
- Stories in the popular press
- PBL problem databases (Appendix 3.4)
- Colleagues outside our disciplines
- Examples and illustrations used in our courses

The transformation of traditional problems to PBL can involve substantial effort, especially when turning simple "plug-and-chug" problems with a single correct solution or straightforward essay questions into open-ended problems. On the other hand, starting with an authentic problem makes the development of a PBL problem less time-consuming because of its inherent lack of structure. Our own experiences are illustrative.

José:

> *The problems I use in my courses come mostly from my own research and consulting experiences and from the problem sets I used to assign students in my lecture courses. I use the former mainly in my upper-level courses in soil microbiology and soil chemistry. They are as real-life as it gets: messy, poorly defined, with more than one reasonable solution, requiring that information from different disciplines be integrated to address the problem—just what PBL is about. From my perspective, I have the advantage of familiarity with all the details of the problem and its actual outcome— I know what was considered, what worked, and what didn't. Writing them did involve some effort, mostly making alterations: simplification, additional data, or changing names to protect privacy. The sample problem in Appendix 3.1 is based on one of my research projects.*
>
> *The problems I use in my introductory soil science class come mainly from problem sets that I had written already. I knew they were difficult (as students were all*

*too happy to tell me), often forcing students to work in (unofficial) groups to solve them. The difficulty originated mostly from the lack of structure that I had built into the problems—they required that students make and justify assumptions and/or use information that I knew they had learned in other courses. So in most cases the transformation to PBL involved placing the problem in an interesting context and ensuring that I was asking open-ended questions.*

Perhaps the richest source of potential PBL problems lies in the examples and illustrations we use to help students understand the concepts and theories of our disciplines. The examples we choose are the result of an intellectual process in which we articulate a concept or theory and then identify circumstances and situations where those ideas can be seen at work. If we turn that process around and begin instead with the circumstances rather than the concept, we are on the way to producing a PBL problem.

C.B.:

*I derived most of the problems I use in my introductory sociology course from materials—examples, cases, and so on—that I was already using in more traditional ways. We often would use a particularly rich example over the course of several weeks, revisiting it periodically to see how different it might seem if looked at from a new perspective or through the lens of a different set of ideas.*

*For example, one of the issues we deal with is the complicated relationship between our desires to construct our own identities and the claims made on us by those groups to which we necessarily belong. I'd used a slightly fictionalized example from a Hutterite community (a communal religious group residing in Canada) to help ground this discussion, but I was doing most of the work. Students would discuss the issue a bit, I'd take a few reports, and then I provided the analysis that made the point I wanted to make.*

*In transforming the example into a problem, I thought about the steps I had taken when I selected the example in the first place. What were the basic ideas I wanted to get across? How did the example embody these ideas? What were the lines of connection between this example and other aspects of the course? I then tried to duplicate that process in the problem, sequencing the questions I posed so that students would think their way through the issues (as I had) rather than have me lead them along.*

*This produced a problem that was, perhaps, a bit more structured than most PBL problems. We did go step by step, but I don't see that as a real drawback. The course is very large and the students are nearly all first-semester students, so a bit more structure may have made the problem more suited to my circumstances.*

PBL is an especially powerful way to link the content of our courses to the world outside the academy. News stories and contemporary events often provide raw materials that can be readily fashioned into compelling PBL problems.

Libby:

*My problems begin philosophically with my course goals, and then I cast about for a topic that would lend itself to the types of public writing I require in my classes. In other words, I really don't have content I need the problem to cover, but rather my aim is to build students' procedural knowledge and encourage a particular attitude about writing. For starters, then, some problems are taken from the headlines. The Indian Ocean tsunami [December 2004] is a case in point. Problems based on this story could be fashioned for almost any course. In fact, a colleague teaching a course in life science used the tsunami as the basis for a whole semester's work, posing problems about disease and sanitation issues, as well as problems that dealt with the complexity of relief efforts and so on.*

*The Congressional internship problem is less dramatic, but it's also a kind of contemporary problem. If I remember right, the trigger was a list of featured speakers on genetics and public policy in a semester-long honors colloquium sponsored by the university. I was looking for an issue that would capture several features I wanted my students to explore and I had this brainstorm that our local Congressman and his position on stem cell research—which at that point was not widely publicized—would be an ideal place to begin. The problem spun itself out from there.*

Reworking course materials or writing problems from scratch is not the only way to produce good problems. There are a number of PBL databases (Appendix 3.4 provides a sampler) that can be accessed with a couple clicks of the mouse. Most sites permit visitors to use the problems that are posted, but it is probably wise to proceed with caution. Even the most elegant of problems has emerged from a context—a particular course, a particular instructor, a particular teaching style—that may not be appropriate for our own purposes. Good problems need to fit our courses, our students, and our styles. Database problems are a good place to start so long as we adjust what we find to fit our circumstances, or perhaps better, use what we find as a springboard to writing our own problems.

## Designing a Successful Problem

The sources of and inspiration for problems can vary, but writing good PBL problems requires some sustained attention to three specific features.

- The *content and concepts* we want students to learn
- The *story* that will keep their attention focused on the problem
- The *structure* of the problem, which makes it open ended and challenging

## Content and Concepts

When we prepare lecture notes, problems, or questions for a course, we start with an idea of what we want students to learn: What do I want my students to understand as they listen to this lecture, work through these problems, or answer these questions? The construction of a PBL problem involves the same sort of thinking: Begin with the end in mind. What do we want our students to learn (run across, run into) as they work through the problem?

More than likely you already have a list of what you want students to learn, whether or not it is in list form. For example, if you are transforming your course (or part of it) from a lecture format to PBL, you already have identified the content students should learn—in your lecture notes. Alternatively, you may have a list of learning objectives for each part of the course, perhaps based on the expectations of an accreditation or professional society. Other good sources of guidance for determining the content of your problem include, of course, your own exams, quizzes, papers, and projects, because these represent what you expect students to know. Finally, textbooks, particularly those for introductory courses, have summaries and/or lists of what the students should learn from a particular chapter. Armed with this information, you now have a good idea of what sorts of things need to happen in the problem for students to learn the content as they work through it.

José:

> *In addition to old problem sets and consulting projects, I rely mainly on my own lecture notes and a list of learning objectives for soil science professionals to determine the content of problems for my introductory*

*soil science course. I also include the objectives I used
in planning the problem as part of the write-up that I
give the students. Although one may argue that this
gives away possible solutions, in my experience this has
not been the case. Rather, the objectives provide them
with guideposts to keep exploration of possible solutions
within the realm of the relevant and generally serve as
a starting point for group discussions (e.g., "So, do you
think this may have to do with measuring the pH of
the soil, since that's one of the learning objectives?")*

Libby:

*All of my writing classes have similar goals, but the
amount of sophistication I expect depends on the level of
the class. Unlike José, I only tell students those goals at
two points: First, on the first day of class, after they've
already gotten knee-deep into the problem, and second,
at the completion of the project, to articulate with them
what they have accomplished and how those practices
will inform their individual work for the rest of the
semester.*

## Story

Problems need to be placed in some sort of context: We want them to
tell a story. It can be a real story, a fictional version of a real story (e.g.,
names, places, quantities changed), or completely made up—
whatever we feel will work best with our students. The stories that
provide the context for our problems are most effective, it seems, if
they address a contemporary issue, have an engaging narrative style,
and perhaps employ a bit of humor.

### Contemporary Issues

Students react positively to problems that address current events
because these problems are relevant to life beyond the classroom.

Furthermore, such problems have already been placed in a larger cultural or societal context. In this respect, PBL problems based on recent news stories or current research and professional practice issues often prove more engaging to students than problems that are merely theoretical in character. The connection between what is to be learned and its application is immediate. There are likely to be few questions about why this or that is relevant when students work on an issue that they have read or heard about elsewhere.

C.B.:

> I have used both abstract—"Let's design a 'good' society"—and much more concrete problems—the wisdom and practicality of reparations for slavery. They both work, but the concrete, contemporary problems have an immediacy for students that the more abstract problems do not.
>
> The reparations problem is a case in point (Appendix 3.2). I created a storyline in which students were asked to develop arguments for and against the idea of reparations for slavery so that the university could take a public stance supporting or opposing the idea. The topic had a bit more than the usual electricity because nearby Brown University had just announced that it had appointed a commission to look into that institution's acquisition of wealth derived from slavery and the slave trade.
>
> The problem is really rich and allows students to find and think about numerous positions, data, and proposals that deal with the effects of race, the consequences of economic inequality, and the moral issues involved in public social policy.

## Narrative Style

One of the goals of PBL is to engage students' interests over a sustained period of time. A narrative style that invites students into the problem can enhance their desire to do the hard work of PBL willingly, even eagerly. One simple way to invite students into the problem is to cast them as the main characters: they have just started a job, were given a new project to work on, or were hired to do a particular thing. As the problem unfolds, each step isn't merely another assignment to be completed. Rather it is something that happens *to them*, and they need to get beyond a snag, find additional information, consult experts, decide what is good data, determine who to believe and which explanations are reasonable.

Libby:

> *The hook I use is to place students in a situation and let them write themselves out of it—I guess you could say that is making them the main characters. They are often employees of a company, or community members trying to get something done despite others' efforts to the contrary. After each phase of the problem, I hand students a reaction to the last piece. "Uh-oh. Your web site has caused some controversy." They then need to dig deeper, find out more, and either figure out some way to control the damage or decide to stand up in the face of controversy. After a bit, they do get leery of turning in something they didn't fully research, because the consequences within our story are rarely good if their work has been sloppy.*

Students often mention that humor is an important aspect of good PBL problems, mainly because it takes the edge off. This is particularly true for students who are not used to the PBL format, or any format other than the traditional lecture followed by exams. A humorous title can engage students' attention right away. Word plays and take-offs on popular TV programs, movies, and books may seem a bit silly, but they tend to be noticed by students. In addition, caricatures, comical situations, and odd references to popular culture can help break down the barrier that tends to keep students from trying to solve a problem. After all, how difficult can a problem be that involves a local, one-hit-wonder 80s rock band?

José:

> *I introduce humor in my problems in the form of exaggerated caricatures of stock characters (e.g., nature-hating developer, tree-hugging student, bumbling boss, corrupt politician, cheating contractor), situations (the know-it-all, crusty old-timer shown up by the seemingly ignorant college grad, the annoying roommate that can't take messages properly), and pop culture references (the millionaire rap artist and owner of a private landfill).*

Using humor in PBL can be tricky. We take the risk that it will assume center stage, with students less interested in the problem than the humor. It may also set the wrong tone with some students, leading them to believe that the course or the instructor or PBL itself is not to be taken seriously. And, of course, humor has the potential to offend students. Obviously, not all problems lend themselves to comic treatment, but some do, and many can be made more engaging with a bit of humor here and there. Although it is not an essential ingredient, used judiciously, humor can make an important contribution to an engaging and successful PBL problem.

## Structure

Because of their unstructured nature, effective PBL problems push students to develop higher-order thinking skills: analysis, synthesis, and evaluation. Solving these sorts of problems gives us and our students a real sense of accomplishment. In addition, open-ended, unstructured problems are often cross-disciplinary, requiring students to move beyond their disciplinary boundaries to get the information they need. This aspect of PBL gives students the opportunity to make connections they may not have attempted otherwise.

Libby:

> *When I teach multiple problems throughout the semester, I like to provide lots of structure in the early ones, then far less later on. The later problems typically offer a scenario with very little information that demands both research and contextual sensitivity. For example, near the end of my business writing class, students will tackle a complicated international shipping and delivery situation adapted from a case written by Mark Schaub at Grand Valley State University, and subsequently published in* Professional Writing Online *[Porter, Sullivan, & Johnson-Eilola, 2003]. Students only know that deadlines are slipping with their supplier in the post-9/11 Middle East during Ramadan. It is their job to find out what that means, and what—if anything—they can do about it.*

There are other advantages of good PBL problems. The cross-disciplinary nature of these problems, in conjunction with the lack of structure and direction, often leads to a considerable amount of group interaction, both to exchange the information students have gathered and to reach a consensus on a variety of questions. These interactions give students an opportunity to develop their skills at presenting information, arguing their case, and examining the validity of ideas.

But there is a balance to be maintained. Problems have to be sufficiently difficult to keep our interest, yet not so difficult that we give up in frustration. One way to adjust difficulty is through the amount of structure and complexity built into both the problem and associated questions. Again, the level and size of a course go a long way toward determining the amount of structure we pack into a PBL problem.

In upper-division courses, where students can be expected to have a solid base of disciplinary knowledge and a developed set of analytical skills, we probably need to worry less about the unstructured nature of PBL than we do about ensuring our problem is difficult and challenging enough to maintain students' interest.

José:

> *One way I keep students challenged is through the judicious use of lies, ambiguity, irrelevant information, and suppression of important data in the problems they work on. For example, I intentionally provide students with erroneous information (e.g., transposed data, wrong terminology, incorrect definitions, wrong equations) in my problems. I do this early on in the semester. It seems to do a couple of things. First, it forces them to trust their judgment with respect to what constitutes valid information. Second, it develops a healthy level of skepticism that keeps them alert throughout the semester.*

Less experienced students are probably not equipped to deal with the muddied nature of problems like those José has described. In fact, even what we think of as well-structured problems can be problematic: Think of students' legendary struggles with word problems. Complex and unstructured problems may be too much to ask of first-year students or students at the beginning of a disciplinary curriculum. Rather than being an appropriate challenge, such problems may overwhelm them.

C.B.:

> *I've got to pay a good deal of attention to structure because my class is so large. If there were fewer students I might be able to manage a less structured problem by visiting groups and asking questions. As it is, with about 100 groups working at once, that's not possible, even when I have help from some advanced under-graduates. So instead, I try to break the problem into chunks by the questions I pose for students. They work on a discrete aspect of the problem in each class session*

*and on another aspect between class sessions. The feedback we give is designed to help them draw the lines of connection between the chunks, so they can see the problem-solving process take shape as their answers to one set of questions lead to the next.*

*I don't worry about this structuring. The questions are still pretty broad—"Which of the 30 articles in the Universal Declaration of Human Rights seem most essential for us to create our own identities?"—and they do require students to think about what they know, what they need to know, and to draw connections between various aspects of the course.*

The more open ended the problem, the greater the risk of students going in unanticipated and unproductive directions in their pursuit of a solution. There is nothing wrong with students exploring blind alleys—figuring out when to give up an unproductive pursuit is part of learning how to solve problems. Sometimes, however, we need to step in to move things along. In general, the more unstructured a problem is, the more aware we need to be of what is going on in our class, intervening in those instances where groups are stymied so they once again can become productive.

## Delivery

As we write problems, we need to consider how they will be delivered: Will students have access to all parts of the problem from the beginning, or will the problem be parceled out over time, first one step, then the next? There are advantages to each of these approaches and which we choose will depend on the level and sophistication of our course and how we have envisioned the timing and rhythm of PBL in our classrooms. Most problems can be delivered either way, but it has been our experience that parceling problems out provides some control and flexibility that make PBL a bit easier to manage.

## All at Once

Delivering all parts of the problem at once often lowers the level of anxiety in students, allowing them to concentrate on the challenges presented by the problem. Students feel better if they know what lies ahead, regardless of how difficult it might be. On the other hand, we lose a significant amount of flexibility as the designers and moderators of the problems. The steps in the problem—usually in the form of questions we pose—are laid out in advance of any proposed solution and are thus locked in, indicating what will come next.

Libby:

> *When I first drew up the Congressional internship problem, I had much more detail in the problem statement. I was interested in stem cell research, abortion, capital punishment—all those "life" issues. I wrote the problem in such a way that all those things would be on the table at once, something like, "Find the Congressman's position on each of these issues and write some campaign literature explaining it to these constituencies." If I had presented the problem that way, I could have directed students' attention to the important issues right away. There would be some advantage in that, but it also would have created a directionality to the problem that I didn't want it to have.*

If we are writing a problem to be delivered all at once, we should keep a few things in mind. First, we should remember that the opportunities to make changes midway through the problem are diminished considerably, so we need to get the story and the steps toward a solution straight from the beginning. Second, we need to be very careful in posing questions to avoid giving away information that we expect students to discover on their own. By phrasing questions in the wrong way, we can inadvertently provide hints to students that can transform a good problem into a much simpler exercise. Finally, because all aspects of the problem are on the table at once, we need to anticipate that different groups within the same class may address aspects of the problem in a different order. We may need a plan to ensure that all our groups work through the entire problem rather than borrowing parts of the solution from other groups who worked on a different part of the problem.

### Phased Delivery

The phased delivery of a PBL problem resembles the problems of real life—seldom do we have the luxury of an omniscient view of a situation, of knowing what the next challenge is going to be. This approach also allows for a more dynamic type of PBL because it allows changes to be made based on the responses of the students to previous sections. In addition, the one-step-at-a-time structure of piecemeal delivery lets instructors monitor more easily the work students are doing on the problem.

C.B.:

> One thing I have tried to do with the questions I pose is to identify places in the problem where students can have enough of an answer to have something coherent to submit. With so many groups working, it is too much to expect all of them to make productive use of class time (or even the time between classes) if all I ask them to do is "work on the problem." Each class session ends with something they need to turn in as a result of their work during the period. Each subsequent session begins with groups submitting the results of their work since the last class session.
>
> This does push a kind of one-size-fits-all process onto the problem, but without it, too many groups would just flounder. Besides, it gives me a quick look inside each group and allows me to make some comments about the directions the answers have taken. It is also, of course, a way of reminding students that the

*& IDENTIFICATION*

> *problem solving part of PBL is as important as the*
> *solution they eventually arrive at—each of the things I*
> *collect is counted toward the grades I assign for the PBL*
> *unit.*

The phased delivery of PBL is a less abrupt departure from ordinary classroom practices than is an all-at-once approach. The often unsettling nature of PBL can be eased a bit by parceling out the problem, even if the problem itself is unstructured (see Appendix 3.3 for an example of phased delivery).

Libby:

> *I give students very little guidance beyond the initial*
> *prompt, but I break my problems into so many phases*
> *that students are rarely at a loss for very long. In other*
> *words, my problems are paced in short bursts, with*
> *"deliverables" almost every class. Those bursts build on*
> *one another, so although I've sequenced it carefully,*
> *students do not feel like I'm telling them what to do*
> *and how to do it. This piecemeal method works in my*
> *classes because that's often how writing tasks are handed*
> *out—with the exception of the academic, research-based*
> *essay. If I sequence their problems with increasing*
> *amounts of new information and different perspectives,*
> *it seems that later in the semester students are able to*
> *transfer those patterns (research, revise, re-research, re-*
> *revise) into their longer academic projects.*

When we parcel out our problems, students do not know what issue will be posed next, how complicated it will be, or how long they will have to complete that phase of the problem. That uncertainty can make the problem more interesting, but it may also produce anxiety, especially among less experienced students. Providing some guidance about the rate and pacing of the phases of the problem is generally a good idea.

José:

> *One approach to the delivery issue that has worked*
> *successfully in my courses is the inclusion of a timetable*
> *(Appendix 3.1). The problem is given in a piecemeal*
> *fashion, but along with the first part of the problem I*
> *include a schedule of when students can expect to be*
> *done with a section and move on to the next. This has*
> *the effect of lowering their level of anxiety, and generally*
> *leads to keeping students on task.*

Whether we decide to parcel out our problem or to present it all at once, we should remember that even the best problems cannot sustain students' attention if they go on too long. As with other classroom practices, variety is important in PBL. The introduction of new problems on some regular basis is especially important in courses where PBL is the sole method of instruction. José likes to remind us that good problems in PBL should resemble Spanish soap operas. Unlike their U.S. counterparts, in which a single plot line can be drawn out unendingly, Spanish soap operas wrap up one plot and begin anew in just a few months. Good problems should be compact enough to be investigated and resolved in a reasonable timeframe so that students can turn their attention to a fresh problem or to another method of instruction.

José:

> *In my courses, work on a problem usually lasts for three*
> *to five class meetings, then it's time to wrap things up:*
> *I ask groups to summarize their solutions and share*
> *them with the rest of the class. In my experience, if the*
> *problems are much shorter, students don't have enough*
> *time to really delve into the problem in a way that is*
> *rewarding. On the other hand, if the problems are too*
> *long, they tend to become tedious.*

Writing PBL problems requires that we pay attention to the content we want students to learn, the story within which the problem unfolds, and the level of structure and complexity of the problem. The bad news is that doing it right requires serious effort. The good news is that the resulting problems are the kind that most students enjoy working on, and watching students learn the content and make connections as they work through them is a very rewarding experience. The next chapter describes how the PBL process unfolds in the classroom.

# Appendix 3.1
# Fecal Follies

## Timetable

| Date | Activity |
| --- | --- |
| 24 October | Work on Part 1 |
| 27 October | Work on Part 2 |
| 29 October | Work on Part 3 |
| 31 October | Work on Part 3; Start Part 4 |
| 4 November | Work on Part 4 |
| 5 November | Presentations |

## Resources

Septic System Fact Sheets, University of Rhode Island Onsite Wastewater Training Center: http://www.uri.edu/ce/wq/has/html/has_septicfacts.html

## Introduction

After the great corn catastrophe of 2003, you decided that perhaps farm living was not the life for you. So you sold the farm to the South County Land Trust and, because you listened to some very bad real estate advice from your brother-in-law, you took a huge financial hit on the sale. You were reduced to begging for your cushy old job at Tiny Solutions. But they didn't bite. Instead they gave you a crappy new job, which is a lot like your old job, except it pays less. It does have benefits, though.

Yours is literally a crappy job. It turns out that Tiny Solutions has been working the septic system angle of the environmental consulting field. The idea came to the president of the company, Mr. Pedro Greenjeans, while reading "Everyone Poops" to his grandchildren. Why hadn't he thought about it earlier? It's so simple: *Everyone poops!* If *everyone* does it, there must be *a lot of it*. And most people want *nothing to do with it*. Add to that the recent news about dead quahogs in Narragangster Bay and fecal contamination of ground and surface water and, BAM: The perfect recipe for profiteering.

Your crappy job involves figuring out how to make money out of this idea. This is going to be hard, since a lot of the easy stuff has already been done: Microbial concoctions that you flush down the toilet and magically improve your system? Done. Potent poop pulverizers? Sooooo last century.

Maybe you should concentrate on the leachfield. You have not heard of any good scams—I mean, plans—involving leachfields. And it seems like you can't swing a cat without hitting a failed leachfield in your Charlestown neighborhood. Maybe something that improves their effectiveness would sell. But what? And what do you know about how a leachfield works? It looks like you are going to need some data. As usual, Tiny Solutions is strapped for cash, so it has very little money for internal research and development projects. You decide to get the data you need from your own septic system. And maybe you'll involve your children. Why not? It would be an educational experience, you'll spend quality time with them, and it'll save you a bundle in personnel costs. Damn, you are good.

## Part 1

You first need to get an idea of how the wastewater changes after it passes through the leachfield. You poke around your backyard and after awhile you locate the septic tank and leachfield trenches. All you were able to round up from the equipment room at Tiny Solutions was a couple of zero-tension lysimeters, which you install so that you can sample water about a foot below the bottom of the trench. You also install a sampling port at the outlet of the septic tank that allows you to sample effluent from the tank. You even manage to train your six-year-old kid to take samples aseptically.

You've got the field aspect covered, but the analyses to be made on the water samples are still up in the air. People are concerned about dozens of things that are found in domestic wastewater. But analyses are expensive ($20–$40 per sample per analyte), and you don't have much of a budget for analytical work.

- What should you analyze for? Why? Where should you sample? How often should you sample?

# Appendix 3.2
# Reparations for Slavery: Paying the Piper

Our higher education neighbor to the north, Brown University, has just begun an inquiry to determine whether it ought to establish some system of reparations because in the past it has benefited financially from the practice of slavery and from the trading of slaves. The University of Rhode Island doesn't want to be left on the sidelines when it comes to dealing with this important issue, so our president has asked us to supply him with well-reasoned recommendations about our university's stance on the issue of reparations for slavery, along with a thorough sociological and philosophical justification for those recommendations. Our work is due to him in two weeks time.

To help us along, he has supplied the following material for our consideration.

## Overview

Slavery was eliminated in the United States in 1865 by the ratification of the Thirteenth Amendment to the United States Constitution. Since then, there has been periodic discussion about how we as a society might address the lingering effects of slavery on society in general and on African Americans in particular. These conversations have often been contentious and, as you are probably aware, they have yet to produce anything resembling a consensus.

In the last few years, there has been renewed interest in the idea of *reparations* as a way of addressing the contemporary consequences of the now-dismantled American system of slavery. Although there were calls for reparations in the immediate aftermath of the Civil War (the famous "forty acres and a mule" proposal of Thaddeus Stevens in Congress in 1867) and throughout the 19th and early 20th centuries, none were enacted into law, and the idea faded from the very limited part of the public square it occupied.

By the late 1960s, the success of what has come to be called the Civil Rights Movement reenergized the discussion of the idea of reparations, and there were a number of resolutions regarding reparations on the agendas of a variety of academic, social, and religious organizations. In addition, a cluster of demands for reparations for other historic injustices emerged—reparations for the survivors of the Holocaust, reparations for Japanese Americans who had been interned during World War II, and reparations for a host of others who had been deprived of both liberty and property by oppressive laws and discriminatory social practices. These demands for reparations had the effect of legitimizing discussion about the idea of recompense for historical wrongs and created a broader context for the consideration of reparations for slavery.

Events in what had once been colonial Africa also had an energizing effect. The dismantling of the system of apartheid in South Africa and the subsequent efforts of the South African government to acknowledge its racist history and to provide recompense and reconciliation to its victims drew new attention to the long struggle by some in the United States to establish a program of reparations to compensate the descendents of those Americans who were held as slaves.

Randall Robinson, the founder and president of TransAfrica, an organization that was formed to influence United States policy in Africa and the Caribbean, has become the best known spokesperson for the reparations movement. Robinson (2000) lays out what he sees as the basis of reparations claims in his most recent book, *The Debt: What America Owes to Blacks:*

> This book is about the massive crime of official and unofficial America against Africa, African slaves, and their descendents in America. No race or ethnic or religious group has suffered as much over so long a span as blacks have—and still do—at the hands of those who benefited, with the connivance of the United States government, from slavery and the century of legal American racial hostility that followed it. Solutions to our racial problems are possible, but only if our society can be caused to face up to the massive crime of slavery and all it has wrought. (pp. 7–8)

Of course, the efforts to develop some system of reparations for slavery in the United States have never been without their critics. In fact, those opposed to reparations have dominated the discussion to such an extent that the consideration of compensation for the descendents of slaves has been confined to the outermost margins of public discourse. Randall Robinson's stature and his willingness (along with several others) to articulate the case for reparations has, at least somewhat, moved the reparations issue closer to the center of the public square.

The new centrality of reparations and the controversial nature of its proposals became clear when in 2001 David Horowitz, a syndicated columnist, attempted to place an advertisement titled "Ten Reasons Why Reparations for Blacks is a Bad Idea *for Blacks*— and Racist Too" in student newspapers at colleges and universities across the country. A number of campuses (including Brown University) were wracked by protests following the appearance of Horowitz's advertisement. Although the arguments swirled around issues of race, free speech, oppression, and sensitivity, there was little substantive discussion of the reparations issue and its relationship to how we make sense of our life together.

## Additional Materials on Our Web Site

I have posted some additional material to spur our thinking about the reparations issue on the course web site. You can view them there, or download and print them to bring to class with you.

- First, you'll find a short statement titled "Restatement of the Black Manifesto." This piece presents the argument that underlies the position in support of reparations. This version of the Black Manifesto (which appeared originally in the late 1960s) has been issued by the TransAfrica Foundation, the organization founded by Randall Robinson.

- Second, you'll find the complete text of David Horowitz's "Ten Reasons" advertisement. Although Horowitz doesn't thoroughly develop each of his points (something also true of the Black

Manifesto), he does cover a wide range of objections to reparations. This is the precise text that proved so controversial upon its release.

- Third, you'll find a somewhat longer and somewhat denser discussion of some of the practical problems of providing reparations. This essay has been produced by an organization called Human Rights Watch and can, I think, be described as supportive of reparations. I have included it here because neither the Horowitz piece nor the Black Manifesto addresses the pragmatic questions that surround any program of reparations.

You should read each of these pieces carefully, paying attention not only to the points they make but also to the narratives they allude to. When you next come to class, you and your group should be ready to begin the PBL process by tackling the following assignment.

## Part I

Make a list of at least six questions you would have to answer before you could make a decision about which of the positions on reparations is correct.

# Appendix 3.3
## Congressional Internships

You have applied for several writing-intensive internships through the University of Rhode Island's Office of Experiential Education, and you have been offered a position in the Rhode Island office of Congressman James Langevin. Because House of Representative terms are only two years, you assume you will be writing campaign materials. You have also been told that you will be working on a team with three or four other writing interns.

## Questions for Team Discussion

- Who is James Langevin? What do members of your team already know about him?

- How long has he been in Congress? Who does he represent?

- What issues seem to concern him most?

- What constituent groups and platform have gotten him elected and reelected?

- What has he done during his time in Congress?

- What do different interest groups think of him so far?

- What more do you think you need to learn about him?

- Where can you go to learn more about him?

# Appendix 3.4
## Sample Internet Resources for Writing PBL Problems

### Problem-Based Learning, University of Delaware:

Advice on how to write effective PBL problems, as well as examples from a wide variety of disciplines

http://www.udel.edu/pbl/

### Problem-Based Learning Faculty Institute, University of California–Irvine:

Sample problems developed by faculty from various disciplines, from humanities to engineering

http://www.pbl.uci.edu/

### National Center for Case Study Teaching in Science, University of Buffalo:

A large collection of case studies in basic and applied sciences

http://ublib.buffalo.edu/libraries/projects/cases/case.html

### Problem-Based Learning, Samford University:

Suggestions and resources for writing PBL problems

http://www.samford.edu/pbl/

### Problem-Based Learning in the Sciences and Liberal Arts, University of Calgary:

A collection of problems in biomedical sciences and liberal arts by a professor of pharmacology

http://www.fp.ucalgary.ca/chari/pbls/index.htm

*Note.* All sites accessed April 2006.

# 4
# Controlling Chaos in PBL: The Messy Middle

Let's pretend: You are now convinced to try PBL. You have developed at least one good problem to try with your students, and you have done some upfront work to create a foundation for productive student work. Now, have at it!

Of course, it is not quite that easy. We cannot simply throw a problem at students and let them go wild without any structure or guidance. Instructors must be both organized and flexible. A solid organization allows more flexibility when issues arise as the students grapple in sometimes unexpected ways with the problem.

This, the messy middle, can be the most exciting part of the course, because this is the time your instructional goals can really pop—when we see and hear students working through the problems, articulating what they know, and stretching themselves to figure out even more. They talk about what they know, and how they know it, teaching other group members how to learn in new ways. They check each other on whether their new knowledge is credible and usable. They offer solutions and test them out, comparing them with what their classmates in other groups devised.

There is an excited buzz to a PBL classroom that functions effectively, but that cannot be left to chance. If PBL is to produce the results we desire, we must attend to how we structure and manage class time, perform as guides and mentors, and support students during this often unpredictable process.

## Conducting Class

The goals of a particular class often determine how PBL proceeds. In other words, based on the level of the class, the overall teaching and learning goals, and the time allotted to the problem, we each have different paths regarding how much structure to establish, what tools we make available in the classroom itself, and how we balance in-class activities with out-of-class work.

## Sequencing

One of our first decisions is where to place the initial PBL problem in the syllabus. There are three basic options—beginning, middle, and end—each with its own benefits and consequences. Starting with PBL from the first day of class can establish a tone of active inquiry, send a strong message to students about how the class will proceed, and cement good work practices from the outset.

José:

> *My courses are all PBL, all the time. So students get started on the first problem the first day of the course. I want them to experience the PBL cycle as soon as possible, so that they begin do it without thinking about it. Jumping right into a PBL problem does not allow students much time to think about whatever objections they may have to this approach. Before they know it, they are sorting out what they think they know, what they need to find out next, and who'll be doing it. Having no other choice but to grapple with the subject matter of the course right away, students become engaged in the learning process.*

Libby:

> *Because PBL encourages a contextual approach to understanding situations, I often use it to set up my course concepts at the beginning of the term—the very first activity on the first day, extending through the first*

*few weeks. Immersion in PBL helps students understand the roles writing can play within different contexts, with different audiences, and for different purposes. In other words, I want students to get quick experience with lots of kinds of writing, revision, and feedback…and then I want them to see that their writing can have social consequences. I've found that their later projects are more powerful if students start practicing writing as an explicitly social action from the get-go.*

Problems in the middle of the course can introduce a new concept to students, allowing them to work their way into a new unit. In this case, PBL replaces the typical lecture time, as students work through the information together for the first time.

C.B.:

*I usually introduce the initial PBL unit right after our first exam. I have thought about starting the course with PBL, but because it is so large, I think students need to get their feet on the ground a bit before we start PBL. Also, the organization of the course makes this an ideal time to introduce PBL. We have just finished setting a foundation for the semester's work and now we are ready to begin more in-depth exploration using what we have learned as a jumping-off point. I decided to use PBL at this point for two reasons. First, I used to pose rhetorical questions to students in my presentations, asking things like "What sort of society do we require if we are to create authentic identities?" Why not pose that as a problem for them to work out rather than one for me to explain? Second, the PBL unit breaks the lecture-then-small-group-discussion rhythm of the course while really emphasizing that the group work we've done is important.*

Another alternative for the middle of the course is to use PBL to extend and apply concepts already discussed in the class, but with new wrinkles introduced. This timing might allow students to pull together several threads from earlier in the semester and use them in a new way for a novel situation. It is worth noting that this approach is more like a case-study than classic PBL, and it runs the risk of having too much of the teaching done for the students ahead of time.

C.B.:

> *I've also used something like PBL to get students to try to apply the ideas we have developed over, say, the first eight or nine weeks of the semester. I don't really ask them to go through the usual "what do you know; what do you need to know; how can you locate and evaluate relevant information" aspects of PBL. Instead, I'll give them a problem or two that pose dilemmas relevant to our previous discussions and ask them to resolve the issues. Most groups make the connections between the issues in the problems and what we have done before, but because they draw those linkages themselves (rather than me doing it for them), their learning seems richer and deeper. I should say that the problems I use for this tend to revolve around a single issue. For instance, I've used three problems about religious practice and gender equality that, when posed sequentially, make it a challenge for students to come to some consistent position across the three dilemmas.*

Finally, as more institutions are encouraging the use of capstone projects (or even entire capstone classes), it makes sense to end the class with an active independent inquiry problem, drawing new insights and applications. Placing PBL at the end of the class is not merely an extension of what students have already learned; rather, it is an opportunity to take their previous knowledge and practices to a different level.

## A PBL Syllabus

In the schedule portion of a traditional syllabus, students have a clear understanding of the course expectations, homework assignments, and due dates for major projects and exams. Clear expectations are often the hallmark of a well-designed syllabus, keeping both professor and student on track. With PBL, the well-designed syllabus is a bit different.

If we tell students what they should read between classes, and what the major topic of the day will be, we may give away much of the problem solving we want them to learn. Savvy students will look to the syllabus and schedule for hints about the next phase of the problem or a suggestion about the next tool to try. There may be good reasons to offer this support, but we like to make sure it is a conscious choice and not an unreflective habit based on years of solid syllabus design.

Libby:

> My students need the predictability of major due dates in their schedule, and they do like knowing there is an end in sight to the project. Particularly with first-year students, I want to support their development of good time management habits, so listing major deadlines is crucial. Having said that, I try to give students very few clues about the middle of the project. This means my schedules show a lot of TBA time in between the major due dates. Because I tend to sequence my projects with many different phases, the end points of each phase are shown in the schedule. This was quite a departure for me; in my non-PBL classes, I spell out each homework assignment in excruciating detail, exhorting students to "check your syllabus" every time they asked what was due.

José:

> *The typical syllabus for my PBL courses includes 1) learning goals (for content as well as skills), 2) a description of the PBL process, 3) a detailed description of assessments (for individual and group work), and 4) a bare bones schedule of activities, essentially indicating the time we will be working on each problem. As mentioned in Chapter 3, I provide the schedule details—which part of the problem we expect to be working on, when papers are due, and so on—as part of the problem write-up.*

C.B.:

> *Because of the size of my course, my syllabus has to carry a heavy load in explaining the ins and outs of how the course will be conducted and managed. Adding an extensive explanation of PBL to an already long document didn't seem to make sense, so instead I added a general overview of the PBL units and promised more information later. I don't think this bothered my students; in fact, it may have piqued their curiosity. When we started the PBL unit, I distributed what amounted to a mini syllabus, including a description of PBL and how we would proceed, as well as a sense of what we could expect over the next couple of weeks.*

## Our Role

Much of our job during this active, hands-on time is to establish each working session by reinforcing the basic inquiry structure of PBL: What do we know? What else do we need to know? How can we learn it?

## In the Beginning

At the start of the semester (or the first problem, whenever it appears), students will most likely need this basic three-part structure reinforced before, during, and at the conclusion of each class. Taking the time to do this—repeatedly—helps lay the foundation for more student independence later in the problem cycle. Allowing ample time for each of these questions early on can be crucial for ensuring that students internalize the inquiry process enough to replicate it successfully on their own.

### What Do We Know?

This first step allows students to begin pooling their knowledge and sets an important tone for the group dynamics to follow. Depending on the level of your students, it may be important to assure them that no information is too trivial for the earliest inquiry. In other words, it is okay to state the obvious when drawn from the language of the problem itself, as this helps other students pay attention to the wording of the prompt. Provide enough time for students to really probe their own knowledge, and enough time for them to get frustrated that they do not know more.

C.B.:

> In the reparations problem, students need time to read the background materials. This takes more time than is available in class, so I ask them to do that reading as homework for the first PBL session. I try to focus their reading by posing the question I want to begin the problem as part of the assignment so they will know what they ought to be thinking about. I don't assign any other reading during PBL units, so this doesn't add to their burden. Most students tell me that they actually do more work outside class during the PBL portions of the course than they do during the "normal" portions.

Libby:

> *I prefer to let students share information as a first step in their groups, although I'm aware of some faculty who like to model information sharing with the full class. As long as I can circulate and help guide each group, each student has a stronger voice in the smaller group than in the full class discussion—especially first-year students, and others who are particularly reticent.*

## What Else Do We Need to Know?

Once students have pooled their existing knowledge, they will find their limits and begin generating questions. Usually, this will happen naturally through their conversation, as students automatically wonder about what they do not know. Professors, then, should be alert to the change in conversation and encourage students to write down those questions as they arise.

Libby:

> *In my first-year classes, I punctuate their conversation with a PowerPoint slide of additional questions, just to help them along after they've tried generating their own questions for a while. I find this can take them into even more questions, provided they understand that the questions I pose are merely generative, and not offered as "the" questions they'll be answering. For my graduate students, I give no guidance on question-forming, since this is one of the most important abilities I want them to develop.*

## How Can We Learn It?

This third step may be where some groups begin to struggle. Many students have preconceived notions of how learning happens, and it is precisely these notions that PBL seeks to disrupt. Some may look for textbooks, and when we have them available in the classroom, we point students in that direction. Students will invariably turn to the Internet to get their questions answered. When approached with sufficient skepticism, the Internet—and especially search engines—can be an excellent source of information. They can also use the Internet to ask questions of experts via email.

Libby:

> *My graduate students, interestingly, have been the most invested in needing (or expecting) to learn directly from the professor. The most resistant class I've taught using PBL routinely asked me to lecture on one subject or another rather than finding ways to learn it on their own, collaboratively. I've found the first-year students are more open to trying their own ways first—a little less grade conscious, a lot more adventurous.*

## Pacing the Class

Although it may not appear well organized to an outside observer, there is a rather predictable temporal structure to most PBL classrooms. As students go through the process each class session, that structure becomes internalized and requires less overt guidance from the instructor at the beginning of each class meeting. Just as in a more traditional class, each session will still have particular goals; in a PBL classroom, however, those goals may well have been set by the students rather than by the professor. This isn't to say that the professor has nothing to do while the students do all the work. On the contrary, a PBL classroom can provide a good aerobic workout as you move from group to group.

José:

> *On the first day of the problem, I begin the class by distributing the printed problem (or I have them download it from the course web site), giving students time to read it silently. I then ask one student to read the Introduction and Part 1 to the whole class. After that, the groups have about 20–25 minutes for discussion,*

*focusing on 1) what's being asked, 2) what do you know that can help you get to a solution, and 3) what do you need to find out to get to a solution.*

not "THEN"

C.B.:

*When we start on a PBL unit, I try to do as little talking as possible. I might summarize the problem very briefly, or I might just say what the issue is and pose the first question or set of questions. After that, students are off to the races. I circulate through the room and dip in and out of various group discussions, noting which ideas seem on track and which do not. Occasionally, I'll stop a group's discussion and make a few comments, interrupt the whole class to clarify a point, or pose a question that will help most of them overcome a common sticking point.*

## From Then On

The beginning of each subsequent class session is a time to reorient the class to the work they have been doing and to focus them on the tasks ahead that day. Even if some groups get to work right away, it can be important for all groups to have some time at the beginning of class to reacquaint themselves with the problem and share their information. This can be particularly critical during times of high stress, for instance, during midterms in their other classes.

Libby:

*Once the project is underway, I will say a few words about what they accomplished during the last session and remind them what they were to bring in today. Most don't need the reminder (it's too late if they do!), but it seems to be a gentle way to get their heads in the right place. Students then begin each class session sharing their homework, determining what they have learned that they didn't know the last time.*

José:

> *The next series of class meetings generally begin with a 10–15 minute period during which I ask students to exchange the information they've collected with their group members. This becomes mostly automatic after the first couple of meetings. Often students purposely get to class early so that they can get the discussion of the new information going.*

Mid-phase pacing can be particularly tricky in large classes, where there is a high likelihood that disparate groups will function at different speeds. As instructors, we may have one pace in mind, only to find out that some groups work far more quickly, while others have difficulty even getting started.

C.B.:

> *As we work through the problem, I open each class with a brief review of the issues we dealt with in the previous session. Part of this review consists of summarizing the agreements and disagreements among the groups or just sampling the class responses as a whole. I'll enter parts of, say, three or four groups' responses into presentation software and show them to the class. I attach the first names of the group members to give the responses a bit of personality. This has a couple of benefits. First, it takes the place of the presentations that often are part of PBL in small classes while giving us all a sense of what others are thinking. Second, and maybe more important, it gives students a sense that they are in a problem together, that someone is reading their work, and that good work will be recognized. You'd be surprised at how pleased they are to have their work displayed for their classmates.*

With the structure in place—what do we know now, and what do we need to know next—group work continues throughout the span of the problem.

## Staying on Task

That deceptively simple phrase—group work continues—can be fraught with difficulty, controversy, and temptation. One of our goals is to have group work continue productively and harmoniously, in keeping with all the best research on collaborative learning. As with all advice on working with groups, there are a number of strategies we use to help students work effectively together and stay on task. Here are some that we use.

- *Make them accountable.* If groups know they will be required to report to the rest of the class at the end of group work, they are more likely to use the time well. Frankly, it is embarrassing not to have something substantial to report, and this is one case where peer pressure can work to our advantage.

José:

> *Once I get a sense that students are talked out, I ask them to stop and have someone from each group report to the whole class 1) what they think is being asked of them, 2) one thing they know that will be useful to answer the questions (and why), and 3) one thing they will need to find out to answer the questions (and why). During this public sharing of information, I ask questions of the reporter (and the group) to help clarify their arguments or to have them consider alternative arguments. I also encourage the class to get involved by asking a group that I know has a different opinion to chime in, or asking the whole class whether something makes sense.*

- *Divide the labor.* If you can, encourage students to divide the tasks so that each person has different information to share that is necessary for the next stage of the project. When students have unique information, they have a compelling reason to use group work and to combine what they have learned. It also guarantees you do not have one student doing the bulk of the work.

Libby:

> *At a midpoint in my Congressional internship problem, I mix the groups up using the jigsaw method [Johnson, Johnson, & Smith, 1991]. I assign different members of each group to research a particular special interest group. Then they report back to their original group (Appendix 4.1). The jigsaw effect comes in when new groups are formed (i.e., one on the right-to-life lobby, one on the American Medical Association) from members of different teams who research and build a new expertise. This shifts the dynamic and provides each member of the original group with a unique contribution to share after the jigsaw is completed.*

Libby's use of the jigsaw is an effective way to create a productive division of labor that remains collaborative, but it can be difficult to manage in circumstances where there are a large number of groups. Left to their own devices, students will often divide the labor among themselves, but they seldom make an effort to ensure that each of them is familiar with every aspect of the problem.

C.B.:

> *One of the problems I have run into is not unique to PBL but a problem with all collaborative group work. What I want to happen is for each member of the group to work on all parts of the problem, sharing his or her information so that the group comes to a true consensus. What often happens instead is that students divide up the problem. One student will do the first part, another*

> *the second part, and another the third part. They then assemble the parts without any real collaboration and without the benefits of the give and take that PBL is supposed to foster. I'm not sure there is a surefire way around this, but having evaluations that focus both on group learning and individual learning seems to be one way. The other thing that helps, I suppose, is to focus on writing real-life, engaging problems. Students often want a say in what their group does if they have a stake in how the problem gets solved because they care about the issues involved.*

- *Limit the time.* Inculcating good work habits while dedicating an entire class session only to group work will most likely be unproductive. "Work days" listed on the syllabus can too often be invitations for procrastination.

Libby:

> *I split the pacing of my class sessions among different elements of PBL. Group work in the first half of each class session can be particularly beneficial—students feel the time pressure in a productive way. They seem to focus more on the task at hand because they know the next task is coming up fast.*

- *Circulate.* Circulating—eavesdropping, really—among the groups is crucial to keeping students moving through the problem.
- *Listen before questioning.* Sometimes we listen without saying a word, then move on to the next group.

C.B.:

> *In a large class, there is nothing more important to the effectiveness of PBL than circulating through groups. Because there are so many at work at once, you can't*

*get to all of them each day, but you can visit some one day, and others the next. Listening to their discussion is an important part of feedback. A nod here or there, a question to clarify, or a brief comment about what another group was discussing can go a long way toward keeping groups working productively.*

José:

*I circulate around the classroom and listen to discussions to 1) get an idea of where things are going, what their misconceptions are, and so on; 2) answer questions (usually with a question that will point them to an answer); and 3) clarify anything that was accidentally left vague in the problem.*

- *Guide only when warranted.* As we suggested, sometimes the best response is to send students back to their groups, to make sure all voices have been heard, and that they are not overlooking something basic.

José:

*When students come to me with questions, I almost always respond with another question: What do you think? This does a couple of things. First, it makes it clear to the students that I am interested in hearing their opinion, which tends to enhance their confidence. Second, and perhaps more important in the context of acquiring problem-solving skills, it forces them to articulate their arguments. Very frequently as the student explains her thoughts, she realizes that either she already knows the answer or where to look for it. Since I ask the question in a group setting, other group members often chime in with their opinion, with the resulting discussion also helping to answer the question or identify a potential source for answers.*

- *Redirect when appropriate.* When you can see that student energy is flagging or that some other direction would serve students better, suggest a change of pace, a walk around the room, or the use of a different resource.

- *Make tools available.* The well-stocked PBL classroom will have most of the tools students need to complete the problem successfully. Some have traditional textbooks for students to use as resources, as well as other reference books and primary sources. Others will have appropriate lab set-ups, with the materials needed for students to run experiments. Yet other features include advanced calculators, computers, ample chalk- or white-board space, and piles of recycled scratch paper. Many of us teach in standard classrooms, where the tools may be limited to blackboards and overhead projectors. Many tools students will already know how to use; others will require more guidance. If there are unfamiliar tools crucial for working through the problem, it will be essential for students to learn and practice with them while they are in the classroom; sending them off to do it on their own can too often lead to failure.

- *Wrap up the class.* Sometimes class just ends. Students are working diligently on their problems, time expires, and students from the next class begin making impatient noises in the hallway. When this happens, the professor's job is merely to nudge students out the door. Most other classes, however, need some shape to the end of their time together, perhaps a chance to articulate what they have just accomplished, an opportunity to bounce their new insights off the other groups, or a time to regroup and redistribute the workload before moving on to the next challenge. Think of this moment as a comma or semicolon in the overall structure of the problem—an opportunity for students to get feedback on where they have been and to anticipate the next step.

C.B.:

*Each aspect of my problem really comes in two parts: one that the groups complete in class and the other that they take with them, to be completed outside class. This creates a pattern in which each group is submitting part of its problem at the beginning (what they took with them and brought back) and end (what they did in class) of each session. On the second day of the unit, I'll summarize what they did in class the first day; after that, we summarize both what the groups did in class and what they did outside class. The summaries lead into a brief introduction to the next parts of the problem, so that where we have been points the way to where we're going. This process keeps the parts of the problem connected so that it doesn't seem like a series of disjointed case studies.*

José:

*In most instances I don't have much to do between sessions, since most of my feedback is provided on the spot, either during intra-group discussions or when groups are sharing their solutions in public. I do try to anticipate the sorts of questions, problems, or directions that may come up in the next part of the problem, and sometimes I make changes in the problem in reaction to what has taken place in class.*

Libby:

*We know from research on writing instruction that faculty feedback is perhaps the most important element of the writing process for most students [Sommers, 1982 & 1992]. With this in mind, I collect a collaboratively revised document from each group at the end of their reporting out and return it the next class with comments and suggestions. Sometimes they are able to incorporate my feedback into the next phase; other times they choose to revise and resubmit. Collecting materials at the end of each class also helps me redirect any groups that are clearly headed in unproductive directions or are enamored with sources that lack credibility for their project.*

• *Wrap up the problem.* The very end of the problem, however, requires more of an exclamation point.

José:

*Once we get to the end of a problem, I ask all groups to give a short summary of their solution. I provide them with an overhead and markers and give them 10–15 minutes to get their information together. This is not as onerous as it may sound, since I ask them to share their progress with the other groups just about every time the class meets. This final rundown helps to identify misconceptions and inconsistencies in their arguments. It also serves as a starting point for the formal presentations and/or papers in which they will present their solution. Having limited space forces them to concentrate on the important aspects of their solution, and having to prepare something that their peers should be able to interpret makes them think about how to present the information effectively.*

## Student Contribution

Although there is much we can do to facilitate and support students during PBL, class sessions rise and fall on the effectiveness of student work. This is both the power and the problem of the method. When students work effectively, eagerly engaging the "what do we know, what do we need to find out" sequence, our classrooms hum with animated conversations that result in thoughtful, well-crafted products. When students are ill prepared, distracted, or disconnected from the problem or each other, PBL classrooms are disorganized, even disorderly, and the products are superficial, even slipshod.

There are a number of strategies to ensure productive group work, and we have mentioned many of them already. The non-traditional nature of PBL, however, makes some of the standard approaches a bit problematic. For example, one generally effective method of keeping groups on track is to specify a particular question that their work should address and answer. In PBL, such a tactic would undermine the basic premise that students should frame and then answer their own questions as they seek a solution to the problem at hand. There is, it seems, an inherent tension between our use of structure to encourage productive discussion and our use of unstructured or loosely structured problems as prompts for PBL units.

We may need to learn to live with this tension by balancing structure and spontaneity, but there are some approaches that can help avoid either spoiling PBL with too much direction or losing control of the learning environment with too little.

## Preparation

Nothing will derail the group work at the center of PBL faster than students who come to class unprepared. Preparing for more traditional instruction (lectures and the like) will enrich students' experiences, but even students who have to do little or no preparation can come away from class having gained something. This is not the case in PBL. Unprepared students can frustrate their more prepared group mates, and, if sufficiently numerous, can effectively block group work. Merely reminding students they need to be prepared during PBL has only a limited effect, but more directive statements about *how* students should prepare for PBL class sessions can pay dividends. One strategy is to ask students to read or reread particular texts or articles (see Chapter 5), making specific mention of how the authors touch on various aspects of the problem at hand. In addition, we might pose questions designed to get students to think about some of the issues posed in the problem. For example, in their work on the reparations problem, C.B.'s students were given announcements of Holocaust reparations programs and news stories dealing with payments to Japanese Americans interned during World War II. Although these articles were not essential to the task the problem posed, they did prompt students to think about the logic of reparations in general, making them more likely to be prepared to engage productively with their group mates. In Libby's classes, students are required to bring a draft of their project using new information generated from their homework; those who come to class empty-handed are glaringly obvious.

## Progress Reports

As we mentioned, one of the tried and true methods for ensuring productive group work is the specification of a product that results from their collaborative efforts. We can, with just a bit of alteration, adapt this same strategy to PBL. As we set the groups to work, we can tell them that we expect a report of their progress or findings in 8 or 15 or 20 minutes. We need not tell them what questions they need to answer or what issues they need to raise; we only need to ask them to be ready to talk about what they have done. In some ways, this "report out" strategy allows the multifaceted nature of PBL to be put on display. Each group has its own agenda, its own approach, and, unlike ordinary discussion feedback that often results in "we had what they had" responses, the PBL progress reports are usually delightfully variable and illuminating.

In large class versions of PBL it is more difficult to use progress reports as a way of keeping students and groups productive. Depending on their number, each group may not be able to report the progress it has made. Sampling groups—asking some to report what they have done at the 15-minute mark, others what they have done at the 30-minute mark—is one way around this problem. Another strategy involves collecting written progress summaries from each group at the end of a class session. The reports can be quickly scanned and briefly summarized at the beginning of the next class session. However we manage it, having groups make progress reports is a good way to keep them productive without cramping the more creative aspects of PBL.

## Keep the Goal Clear

The relatively unstructured nature of much of PBL classroom work makes it difficult for students to remember just what it is we are after. Unlike a lecture where points follow one after the other in some coherent fashion, PBL often proceeds in fits and starts. As students work on this piece of the solution and then that, we have discovered that it is useful from time to time to remind them how each step fits into the larger process of problem solving. We might begin a class session by reminding them of the basic problem that began the unit and recapitulate the progress that has been made toward a solution. It is relatively easy in PBL to get involved in the process and lose sight of the cognitive aspects of the problem. A few well-timed "where we are" reminders can help students see what they have accomplished so far, giving them a clearer sense of what yet needs to be done.

## Trust but Verify

PBL depends on effective group work. Because of that we are often tempted to step in to ensure that each group works, that each student contributes, and that the problem gets solved in a way that all our goals are accomplished. But we should resist the temptation. Students need space to learn, to make mistakes, to get bogged down, to recover and move on if PBL is going to work as intended. We need to give them that space even if, from time to time, it seems inefficient and even ineffective. Nevertheless, we cannot simply turn students loose with a blithe "When you have solved the problem, let me know." We need to trust that our planning, our problems, and our procedures will facilitate student learning with only a little direction and encouragement from us. But we need to verify—evaluate—that all is working as we had hoped.

# Appendix 4.1
# Writing Internship: Before Day 1

What do you know about Jim Langevin?

For our next class:

- As a group, discuss what you know in the group discussion area. Pool your knowledge.

- Before class, each *intern* should post a one-page *fact sheet* about Langevin, and bring to class.

- During the first part of the next class, each intern *team* will combine and revise the individual fact sheets into a team two-pager suitable for presenting to the class.

## Langevin Internship: Day One on the Job

Welcome to your Internship!

- Loaded with good information about who Jim Langevin is, you arrive at the Rhode Island office ready to work.

- An aide meets with the interns for the first day and announces that your team will be assigned to research and do "behind the scenes" work on the *embryonic stem cell* controversy.

- Not sure what this means, your team begins to work.

Remember: You were chosen for this assignment because of your *rhetorical* ability.

- Your sensitivity to different audiences

- Your understanding of contextual complexities

- Your compulsion to research thoroughly

- Your ability to negotiate diverse public perspectives with respect

Questions for Team Discussion:

- What do you already know about embryonic stem cell research? What is it?

- What is Langevin's position on it? How far does his position reach? What are its limits?

- What more do you need to know about his position? Where can you find credible information?

- How have his different constituent groups responded to his stance?

For the next class:

- As a *group*, find out what you need to know about stem cell research, and start researching the answers.

- Each individual *intern* writes and posts a one-page "Langevin on Stem Cells" fact sheet.

- During the next class, each *group* will combine, compile, and design a fuller "Langevin on Stem Cells" fact sheet suitable for public consumption.

*We put your stem cell information on the web...*
*Uh-oh!*
*Information backlash?*
*Or not the kairotic moment?*

What happened?

- Some of Representative Langevin's strong supporters feel betrayed by his public statements in support of embryonic stem cell research.

- Others didn't know his stance, assuming he was strictly pro-life.

- Still others didn't know he was a pro-life Catholic, and now can't believe they supported him in the last election.

What do we do?

- The Langevin team now must do some damage control with different constituent groups. This will require research.

- The new plan is to deploy the intern teams as "Langevin Liaisons" to visit different constituent groups. You have been randomly assigned to these new teams.

- Your job, as a liaison, is to listen respectfully to the concerns of the group, to work toward understanding their issues, to smooth ruffled feathers if possible, and to offer feedback regarding Langevin's position if appropriate.

Challenges for Langevin Liaisons:

- You do not get to choose your own constituent group, so you may be put in one whose interests, values, and ideologies do not match your own.

- If this happens, your rhetorical sensitivity will be all the more important. If you are to effectively listen to their concerns, and learn from them, you may have to suspend your own opinion.


## Langevin Liaison Assignments

Questions for Liaison Discussion:

- What do you already know (or think you know) about this group? What are the names of the organizations you will need to research and contact?

- What are the major philosophies, ideologies, and issues of this group? Where are they coming from? What do they value?

- Where are there divergences and differences within the group?

- What political power do they hold? How might they help or hurt Langevin in the future? How have they in the past?

Reporting back to your intern team:

- With your liaison group, draft an informational report containing what you have learned about your interest group.

- Tailor that draft to fit the needs and expectations of your original Langevin team. What do they need to know about your interest group?

- What recommendations will you make to your group with this new information?

## Regrouping: Negotiating Public Perspectives

Regrouping, continued:

- Meet with your original Langevin intern team.

- Share the reports of what you learned from your interest group.

- Create a plan of action that takes all four perspectives into consideration.

## Last Day of the Internship

- Revise the information and design of the "Langevin on Stem Cells" portion of the web site to reflect your new plan of action.

- Enjoy the satisfaction of a thoughtful job well done!

# 5

# What Now? Evaluation, Revision, and Reflection

So here you are. You have written a problem or two, revamped and reorganized your presentations and your classroom space, mentored, modeled, and guided. How do you know if it all worked? Did your students learn anything? Did your course work in the way you hoped? Given all the effort, does PBL offer a sustainable alternative to more familiar ways of teaching and learning? We suggested ways to think about some of these issues in Chapter 2, but evaluation *in* PBL and evaluation *of* PBL require a good deal of thought and some sustained attention.

It is useful to think about the issues of evaluation in PBL along three axes. First, we must consider how to evaluate student learning. The unorchestrated nature of the classroom, the centrality of group work to the learning process, and the sometimes unpredictable twists and turns on the path toward a solution pose problems that we do not often confront during the evaluation phase of more traditional approaches to instruction. Second, we need to judge how well PBL worked for us—for our course and our objectives—and to reflect on our multifaceted role as author, tutor, and manager, and more. Finally, we need to think about PBL as an instructional strategy, not only in light of our own experiences but also with an eye toward research-based evaluations of its effectiveness.

## The Students

In PBL, students encounter course material (in the form of problems) in groups, they work toward solutions in groups, and they submit their finished work as a group. Yet we also expect that individual students will master and learn to apply the content of our disciplines as a result of their participation in those collaborative efforts. As we noted in Chapter 2, our evaluation of student performance must take into account both the collaborative and individual aspects of the PBL process.

## José's Evaluation Approach

Evaluation in José's full-on PBL approach strikes a balance between collaborative and individual learning. Approximately half of the grade assigned to a student is associated with an evaluation of his or her individual efforts, with the rest based on the products of collaboration. Individual evaluations are based on examinations that students work on individually as well as in groups, with a small fraction of the test grade based on the group effort. José evaluates collaborative contributions through presentations, in which students are asked to explain and defend their solution to a problem, and in synthesis papers, which contain a more structured, detailed exposition of the problem, their solution, and suggestions for future work. He also uses an anonymous peer-evaluation process that adjusts individual grades to reward students who contribute successfully to the process and to penalize those who do not. José's evaluations follow the conclusion of each problem.

## C.B.'s Evaluation Approach

The evaluation process in C.B.'s large class PBL units depends on both individual and collaborative products. The evaluation system he uses mimics the process in other non-PBL units in the course. As they work on the problem, student groups submit a portion of their work at the end of each class session and take another portion as homework to be submitted at the beginning of the next class session. The in-class submissions are counted in a running accumulation of points earned on writing-to-learn activities, with each participating student receiving credit. The homework portions are also recorded as the result of collaborative work—each participating student receives credit—but the points are credited on the examination that concludes the PBL unit. The exam itself is a collaborative effort in which groups can work together, but students remain responsible for their own answers by submitting individual answer sheets. The evaluation process rewards collaborative efforts, but also reminds students that they are ultimately responsible for their own learning.

## Libby's Evaluation Approach

In most of Libby's classes, evaluation is based on process and product; the same holds true for the PBL portions of her courses. The PBL component typically comprises 15%–20% of the final grade, of which half is the group grade for the final *product*. The other half is the *process* grade, which includes both group and individual effort. For the individual effort grade, she relies heavily on the peer evaluations students complete based on a rubric they design in the early days of the semester, supplemented by her own observations of the groups during class time. For the rest of the semester, the remaining 80%–85% is also shared between process grades which are ongoing throughout the term, and product grades as earned in a final portfolio of what students consider to be their best individual writing projects.

As you can see from these summaries, we have designed different ways to evaluate student learning as the result of PBL. Some of those differences reflect the content, level, and size of our courses; others are a consequence of personal style and choice. In spite of their differences, however, our approaches share a crucial feature: We each acknowledge the collaborative nature of PBL while evaluating the learning and contribution of individual students. Balancing collaborative efforts with individual learning is always a challenge, but often that aspect of our evaluation of student performance is relatively minor, confined to a project or presentation that is overshadowed by examinations or other more traditional measures of student achievement. In PBL, however, collaborative learning is all there is, and the need to evaluate individual student learning while acknowledging group performance and contribution requires constant attention.

## Group Performance and Contribution

For most students, the group work involved in PBL is not new, although it may be more extensive than they are used to, especially in full-on PBL courses. Some students will worry about their own participation (*Am I contributing enough?*), while others will be more concerned about the behavior of their collaborators (*Am I going to be left holding the bag?*). Students' previous experiences with group work clearly affect what they expect from the collaborative aspects of PBL, a fact that we think makes paying attention to the connections between individuals and groups worth our while.

### *Acceptable Behavior*

Because PBL groups are durable, lasting a few weeks or even for an entire term, having a clearly articulated understanding of what students owe to one another is an important first step to effective collaboration. One popular approach is to have students develop their own code of group conduct at the outset of the PBL process. This strategy provides students with the opportunity to reflect on and articulate what they value about group dynamics. The fact that the rules are developed by the students themselves can also increase their buy-in, making it more likely that they will abide by their own code. Alternatively, instructors can provide students with a set of expectations for group behavior. This approach leaves less to chance and allows us to highlight those aspects of group participation and conduct that we regard as most crucial. Whichever approach we use, it is important that the expectations for group behavior be made clear as early in the term as possible, setting the tone for the rest of the course.

Libby:

> *Well-functioning groups are so crucial to my classes that I take the time in the first week of class to introduce a mini-case to generate guidelines for group behavior and set expectations for productivity (Appendix 5.1). This is all the more important when I teach first-year, first-semester students in their first-ever college class; some*

*students come from high school with excellent experiences in group work, and others are still scarred from working with dysfunctional groups. The mini-case begins with a description of a peer group that functions well in some ways and not so well in others. My students read that story and use it as a basis for establishing ground rules for the class. What do we want to implement that worked well for the group in the story? What can we institute to avoid the difficulties that group had? What have we learned from previous group experiences that we want to replicate or avoid now? Each group in my class comes up with their own list of guidelines, reports out, and then the whole class discusses the merits of the combined lists. Finally—and this step is the most important for assessment purposes—I take the agreed-upon guidelines, print them, and distribute them during the next class session in two forms: one as a one-page reference list, and one as a rubric they'll use to evaluate each other at the end of the project or semester.*

C.B.:

*I spend some time reminding students to be good group citizens, and I underscore that reminder by asking each group to submit a signup sheet that lists the names and email addresses of the members. Although I cannot really ensure that each student in each group does his or her part, the signup process does, I think, make each student and each group "visible" to me so they have at least some sense of my supervision. And, of course, I have some assurance that they have at least exchanged email addresses.*

## Feedback

Students get feedback on their performance as group members from us and from their peers. As we circulate around the classroom listening to the discussion in different groups, we might encourage participation from a shy student, arbitrate between feuding group members, or discourage unproductive or distracting behavior. Our interventions provide some students with a real-time check on their behavior and remind them that we care not only about the final PBL product but also about the process along the way. Our circulation and occasional intervention are helpful in keeping groups functioning and on track, but nothing is more powerful in the mind of students than the opinions of their peers.

C.B.:

> *I ask the groups in my course to be self-regulating. The work they submit is to list only those members who participated in its production. I think this works reasonably well. Most groups work pretty effectively and as a consequence list all their members all the time. A significant number of groups do, however, omit the names of those students who haven't made a contribution. That feedback, combined with my reminders that "the more you contribute, the more you get back," does seem to make the vast majority of groups work pretty well.*

## Peer Evaluation

Peer evaluations are an effective way to provide students with a concrete assessment of their performance as group members. Although there are a number of ways to structure peer evaluations for PBL groups, we have found that effective peer evaluations in the context of PBL incorporate at least three features. First, as much as possible given the small size of PBL groups, peer evaluations should be anonymous. The anonymity not only frees up student expression, but it also prevents the process from descending into personal quarrels. Second, peer evaluations should be frequent, perhaps at the end of a particular stage of the problem or on a more regular, maybe weekly, basis. Frequent feedback from their peers gives students an opportunity to alter their behavior before serious problems develop. Finally, the peer evaluation process should actively encourage constructive feedback, including suggestions for making the group work more effectively. Positive suggestions for improvement increase the likelihood that students will act on— rather than just stew over—the evaluations of their peers.

Libby:

> *When the final phase of the problem has been submitted to me, I redistribute the rubric that the students developed earlier. Students fill out one per group member, I collate the responses, and use them as part of their process grade.*

José:

> *I ask students to provide an anonymous evaluation of their peers at the end of every problem—after the assignments for that problem have been turned in (Appendix 5.2). They get a copy of the evaluation form at the beginning of the semester so that they know from the start what they are evaluated on: attendance, preparedness, contribution to group discussions, listening skills, willingness to do out-of-class work, and their contribution to group organization and reaching a consensus. Students are encouraged to provide written comments on all evaluations, and they are required to back up poor and outstanding evaluations with written reasons. Since I circulate frequently among groups, I get a pretty good picture of who is doing what, where, and when. Every student gets a summary of the evaluation, along with an edited version of the comments. Most students are hesitant to heap scorn on*

*their fellow group members for minor transgressions. However, egregious violators do get the message very quickly and tend to change their ways for the next problem. On the other hand, those students whose contributions were beyond the call of duty get their due praise.*

## Accountability

To be effective, collaborative work must develop a sense of positive interdependence (that students can only succeed by working together), and it must require individual accountability. Without accountability for their own contributions and their own learning, the temptation for free-riding may be too much for many students. This sort of accountability in a group setting often takes the form of assigning some value for an individual student's contribution to a graded product of group work. This can be done by providing students with the opportunity to distribute a limited set of points among group members based on their contribution. For example, 20% of a project grade can be reserved for peer assessment. Students assign points to their group mates based on their judgment of how much they contributed and how valuable their contributions were. Regardless of the vehicle used, individual accountability gives group members a sense that the process of assigning grades for group work is a fair one—it rewards students who collaborate well and penalizes those who do not. From the point of view of the student being evaluated, the potential impact on grades provides a material incentive to be a good contributor to group work.

C.B.:

*My groups tend to regulate themselves, effectively awarding or deducting points by indicating authorship on their submissions. Occasionally I have had to intervene in groups where free-riding had gone beyond students' capacities to deal with. For instance, students have come to me and said things like, "We waited for them to do their part and they never did and now we're not finished. What can we do?" I typically resolve these problems by splitting the group in two, with one new group being composed of the [I hope formerly] free-riders.*

José:

*Each item in the peer evaluations I use is assigned a value that ranges from 0.70 to 1.05 (Appendix 5.2). I take the average score the student received from all group members and multiply it by the grade the group received in an assessment (say, a paper) to determine the individual's grade. Often one poor evaluation is enough to bring someone back in line. I can think of only a couple of instances in which poor evaluations did not bring the person back into the fold. These individuals ended up getting completely ostracized: cut off not only from group activities involved in solving the problem, but also from those that could be helpful to them, such as study groups and meetings to prepare papers and presentations.*

## Individual Learning in PBL

Evaluating what students have learned fairly and accurately is a complex challenge, and the group aspect of PBL tends to magnify the issue. Not only do we have to contend with the question of assessing individual learning and group efforts, but we also need to balance the relative importance of the collaborative and individual aspects of the process. For PBL to succeed, group work must be taken seriously by students. They must have a sense that the products of group efforts—the solution developed in the process, the ability to collaborate effectively to accomplish a goal—are worth it. Further, they must also understand that without the efforts of their peers they could not have accomplished as much as they have. In this regard, students need to be assured that their group has succeeded and that they, as individuals, have learned what they were supposed to. Students are motivated by grades, so assessing individual and group efforts for mastering course content, as well as rewarding students for working effectively in a group setting, are important aspects of implementing PBL successfully.

The end product of a PBL problem can take many different forms: a paper or presentation describing the solution, a memorandum to a government agency with suggestions to address a pressing issue, or materials for an advertising campaign. Although the type of product dictates the specifics of ensuring meaningful group participation, we have found the following to be helpful.

### Writing Projects

Strategies for working on group writing projects tend to fall into two categories: 1) one student serves as editor, splicing together the contributions of their peers, and 2) one student does the bulk of the writing, with fellow group members making suggestions for improvement. Both provide group members with the opportunity to reflect on the work they have done and to make a meaningful contribution to the final product.

Ideally, the product of either strategy is the result of the fair and earnest efforts of every group member. Even under the best of circumstances with the best intentions, students working on group writing projects face a number of obstacles. The main problem with both of these strategies is that they require a level of planning and coordination generally not found even among faculty members. In addition, the editor tends to benefit most from reflection and integration of the information, but there is a risk involved if his or her group members are uncooperative. One approach to promote group involvement in written assignments is to have a limited number of points assigned to the paper, to be distributed among group members. Individual group members assign a point distribution, with the average number of points awarded to each member. Another approach is to have more than one student in charge of editing or writing, with others being in charge of revisions.

This provides more opportunities for all group members to reflect on the content learned and how it fits within the solution.

Libby:

> *Each phase of my problems ends with some form of writing. Each new phase then requires rethinking and revising in light of new information or a new audience with different expectations and values. At every step, each student is required to complete some version of the writing as homework, then share and revise in class with colleagues. By the time we've made it to the final product of the problem, all students have been drafting and revising along the way. The final day of the final draft, most groups are sitting around the same computer screen deciding what to include, what to cut, what to add that is fresh, and how to design the final document. I don't usually need to help allocate jobs for them at this point.*

José:

> *At the end of every problem, students in my courses produce a group paper. At the beginning of the semester I provide them with a rubric describing my expectations for these papers. They also know that they have the opportunity to revise their paper to earn a better grade. I give them lots of feedback on the paper when I grade it. One student is in charge of the initial version of the paper, and a different student is in charge of revising it. This spreads the burden as well as the opportunities to reflect on what they learned working through the problem.*

## Presentations

Like writing projects, putting together an oral presentation requires students to reflect on what they have learned, integrate this knowledge within the framework of the problem, and to express it so that others can understand—and be persuaded by—their arguments. Presentations have the additional benefit of real-time interaction: All group members are available to expand on and defend their arguments. However, as with writing projects, encouraging fair contribution from all group members can be a challenge. One way to address this issue involves having all students participate in the presentation, taking turns to expound on different aspects of the problem and their solution.

José:

> *Presentations are an integral part of my upper-level courses in soil chemistry and microbiology. Every group has to give a formal presentation describing their approach and solution to the problem. In addition to forcing students to combine their thoughts in order to figure out what they are going to tell the rest of the class, it helps them to write the paper they have to turn in a few days after the presentation. I have tried both having a single student give the presentation and having different students present different aspects of the problem and solution. The latter seems to be preferred by most students because it takes the dreaded spotlight off the individual and spreads the responsibility among all group members. In either case, I expect all members of a group to answer questions—from me and from the audience—at the end of the presentation. The group grade assigned to the presentation includes a significant component (~20%) for participation of group members in answering questions. Because they know this ahead of time, students are aware that they need to be sufficiently knowledgeable of all aspects of the problem to answer questions on the spot.*

Libby:

> *Too often, students suspect their writing containing their best thoughts on the subject to date goes into a vacuum to be read only by the professor and never heard from again. To mitigate this, and to illustrate the range of variation in solutions to the same problem, the final day of the problem concludes with presentations of the final document. Students highlight the choices they made and discuss their reactions to the differences they notice.*

## Exams

Along with group assessment, most of our PBL courses evaluate individual learning, usually in the form of exams. Individual assessments are an important component of the pedagogy within the structure of group-oriented courses. First, they provide you and the student with a sense of what was learned. But beyond the obvious benefits of the feedback generated by individual learning assessments, they also act as checks on the system. They encourage students to not rely solely on their peers but rather do their own learning. For students averse to having their grades depend on the vagaries of group dynamics, individual assessments provide a degree of control over their grade.

José:

> *I give take-home tests in two parts. The first part is done by the student individually. When the tests are turned in, I give them the same test to work on as a group during class. The final test grade is weighed heavily toward individual effort (about 80%), with the rest based on group effort. This gives students an opportunity to show their individual mastery of course content, especially when they have to explain their answers to the rest of the group. In cases where their understanding was faulty, they benefit twice from the*

*interaction with their peers: They correct their misconceptions and they get additional points in the test.*

C.B.:

*My PBL units always conclude with an exam on which the PBL working groups are permitted to collaborate. Each student has an individual answer sheet but during the exam the groups talk among themselves about the questions, the correct answers, or whatever else seems appropriate. The process is relatively simple but it does allow students to benefit from collaboration while taking responsibility for their own answers. Students can also keep their thoughts to themselves if they wish— another way of dealing with group mates who may have been less helpful than I hoped. In addition to this in-class exam, there is also an out-of-class portion that depends on group work submitted regularly throughout the PBL unit. The group work accounts for between one-third and one-half of the points available on the PBL unit exam. This ratio has been reasonably effective. It encourages groups to work diligently between sessions but it also asks individual students to take some responsibility for their own learning during the exam itself.*

## Weighting

C.B.'s comments about the distribution of points between group work and individual answer sheets raises another issue for the PBL evaluation process: the relative value we assign to group and individual efforts. For the most part, we find that it is best to err on the side of giving students more control over their grade. We tend to place slightly more weight (>50%) on the results of individual efforts. This gives students a greater feeling of control over their final grade, ameliorates some of the anxiety generated by the unknown of group grades, and cuts down on the effects of free-riders. The alternatives are not very appealing. A PBL course in which none of the grading is based on the products of group work sends the message that such work really has no value—why bother, then? On the other hand, the absence of individual assessment not only promotes parasitic behavior, it leaves the students without a clear idea of what—or whether—they learned anything in the course.

## What Worked—and What Didn't

Because of the nontraditional nature of PBL, evaluating its success is especially important. You want to be sure that students have acquired the substantive knowledge of the discipline, but you also want to assure yourself that even though you did not lecture, the course worked. Sources of feedback on what did and did not work in your PBL problems are many, and each conveys important information to be reflected upon as you assess and revise the content and structure of the problems and, in some cases, the course.

### Assessing Problems

As we discussed in Chapter 3, successful problems catch—and retain—the interest of students, keeping them focused on the content we want them to learn. There are many clues to whether this is true of your problems. As you circulate among groups, pay attention to the level of discussion. Do they frequently look like they have nothing to say? Does discussion end early in the session? Do they stay on task? Are the conversations mostly off topic? Are they focusing on trivial or tangential aspects of the problem? You also want to ask the same questions of the discussion at the class level, when groups are reporting on their findings or presenting parts of their solution to the whole class. These daily interactions provide you with a wealth of useful feedback on the effectiveness of your problem. Yet you want to keep things in perspective—even when students are working on the most effective, engaging problem, there will be the occasional long, awkward silence and the bad day. Start thinking seriously about revising your problem when most class meetings show symptoms of bored, off-track students.

José:

> *One clear sign that students are interested in a problem is that their perception of class time changes. Students engaged in solving a problem frequently show up to class early to start discussing the information they gathered since the last meeting. And they often stay—inadvertently—after class has finished. You don't hear the slamming of books and shuffling of backpacks 10 minutes before the end of class: the sounds of students anxious to get away from that class.*

C.B.:

> *I have been consistently surprised at the length of students' written responses to various steps in the PBL process. Although I often suggest guidelines—"To address this aspect of the problem adequately, your group will need to write three or four paragraphs"—many, many groups exceed them. The extra length may not be an indication of the quality of their thought—though it often is—but it does, I think, provide pretty compelling evidence that the problem has engaged them.*

While listening to group and class discussions indicates whether students are on the right track with respect to mastering the content of the course, properly designed assessments—tests, papers, presentations—can give you a more concrete idea of what your students are—and are not—learning. One way to determine whether the learning objectives are being met is to devise a list of concepts you want students to learn from a particular problem ahead of time. Ideally, you will have drawn this list in the process of writing a problem, as suggested in Chapter 3. This allows you to figure out the areas that were successfully covered working through the problem, how well the students understood the concepts, what sorts of misconceptions they developed, and what needs to be improved.

C.B.:

> *One of the changes I have made in my PBL units is to assign companion reading as we work our way through the problem. When I started, there was no assigned reading during the two-week PBL unit, just in-class and out-of-class work on the problem. As a consequence, the content of the problem, although interesting and engaging, seemed disconnected from what we had done before and what we would do after. The reading is not overly long but it is related to the problem without directly addressing the issue I have posed. In a sense, it is an "owner's manual" for the problem that students can use to get ideas about what might come next. Additionally, the reading serves to remind students that the group cannot do everything that needs to be done.*

## Revising Problems

Improving PBL problems can take many forms. One extreme involves completely scrapping the problem and starting from scratch. Some problems are so fundamentally flawed that this is the only reasonable thing to do. If you decide that your problem is fixable, look at both the structure and content of the problem as areas for improvement. Changes in the sequencing of events, length of each part, and pacing can often make a big difference in the way a problem is received by students. Similarly, altering the context in which information is presented and how it is requested can lead to significant improvement in a problem.

José:

> *I had to kill a problem I wrote when I first converted my soil microbiology class to a PBL format. It simply did not work: The writing was boring (it started with*

*a discourse on the molecular composition of microbial cells), and it provided no context for why this was of practical importance, so students were understandably unenthusiastic about identifying the factors that determine the carbon-to-nitrogen ratio of micro-organisms. Rather than try to dress it up, I scrapped the problem and incorporated the concepts I wanted students to learn from this problem into a problem involving nutrient cycling in food webs. It wasn't easy to let it go—all that time and effort—but it had to be done.*

Libby:

*One summer, I designed a problem I was just sure would perfectly capture the spirit of one of my graduate courses, offering a chance for graduates to bridge theory and practice by thinking through (and learning how to research into) real problems that arise at real universities. In my heart of hearts, I still believe this problem was written well, but for various reasons it didn't work in this graduate class. How could I tell? One of their instructions was to locate a department in which the opening "problem" memo could have been written, and every group created their own fictitious department! When my strong feedback indicated that they should use, instead, one of the many institutions at which they were all teaching, all but one group still refused to do so. The resulting solutions were works of fiction and did little to extend their understanding of the course's theoretical readings. I'm still sad about letting go of that one, and I may continue to look for the right situation in which to pull it out again, and revise it appropriately.*

## Recycling Problems

Whether to reuse, refurbish, or write new problems is a constant part of the evaluation of PBL courses. The answer usually boils down to the nature of the problem and the students who are taking the course. Problems that involve a hot issue grab students' attention, but we find that they also tend to get stale fast. We have to toss them after using them two or three times. Finding another hot issue around which to craft a problem that addresses the same content usually is not a problem. Classic problems—those that address time-honored issues in a field—tend to persist longer. Adjustments to these types of problems often involve changes in the storyline or context-specific variables to keep them current.

Our experience has been that required and general education courses taken by large numbers of students necessitate that problems be rotated. To this end, instructors might develop two or three problems that address the same content and alternate them between semesters. This may be a less effective but more practical solution than writing new problems each term, and it does tend to reduce the temptation for students to pump those who have already taken the course for information that may help expedite the problem-solving process.

Libby:

> *There were so many reasons to like the Congressional internship problem (Appendix 3.3) I used with my first-year writing students, not the least of which were that nobody knew very much about him, and he'd kept his position on certain issues (like stem cell research) pretty well hidden. Then came the 2004 Democratic National Convention, at which Representative Langevin spoke very clearly about his position. Now, my problem no longer worked in the way it had before, because a simple Google search brought the answer in seconds. I've been fiddling with ways to revise the problem to make it more difficult to get to the initial*

*information, but so far I've had only limited success. Ultimately, I may need to write a whole new problem about a different social issue.*

C.B.:

*One of the more useful ways to deal with problems becoming too familiar is to alternate content-rich problems with more abstract versions addressing the same issue. The reparations problem is a good example of a content-rich approach: There is plenty of information to be had that is specific to reparations for slavery in the United States. The question embedded in the problem—what responsibility do the members of a society have to right the wrongs of the past—can also be extracted from the specifics of reparations and posed independently or be embedded in a different (perhaps even imaginary) setting. By changing from concrete problems to more abstract versions (and back again), the problems can maintain their freshness and the course can maintain its continuity from semester to semester.*

## The Sustainability of PBL

Our own reflections about what has worked in our PBL units and what hasn't need not be entirely introspective. We can augment our own thoughts with data collected from students. Although nearly all institutions have established systems for collecting student evaluations, it is probably not a good idea to rely solely on them. Most standard student evaluation of teaching forms (including those used by our institution) are geared toward more traditional classroom interactions—lectures interspersed with discussions and other activities. As a result, they are not likely to provide insight into student reactions to the very different nature of PBL.

It is relatively easy to develop a set of questions focused on the dynamics of PBL that can be administered to students following the conclusion of a PBL unit or even at the end of a full-on PBL course (perhaps in conjunction with the institutional system of student evaluation). The following questions can provide a wealth of information to supplement (or even correct) your own sense of how well things worked:

- Compared to how courses are usually conducted, how do you rate problem-based learning?

- How well do you think your group worked during problem-based learning?

- How much did you learn during the problem-based portion of our course?

- What made you rate your experience as high as you did?

- What kept you from rating it higher?

C.B.:

> I have collected nearly 1,500 responses to a series of questions I pose to students following the completion of our PBL units. The questions are pretty simple, but the responses are revealing. Students clearly enjoy the PBL portion of the course (70% rate it "much" or "somewhat" better than our usual class sessions) and they also are pleased with the productivity of their groups (80% rate that "excellent" or "good"). More important from my perspective is the fact that two-thirds of them say they do more work between classes during PBL than they do during our more traditional units. Many also report learning "a lot" (more than one-third) and more than 80% rate their PBL experience as "excellent" or "good."

José:

> *In conjunction with my colleague—who also teaches*
> *introduction to soil science using PBL—we have polled*
> *the students in our courses [Amador & Görres, 2004].*
> *As was the case for C.B.'s sociology class, our results*
> *indicate our students had a positive experience with*
> *PBL. Nearly 90% of students reported that their group*
> *worked "well" or "very well." About 70% thought that*
> *PBL was a more effective vehicle for learning than*
> *lecture. The majority of students also felt that the PBL*
> *format had helped them improve their problem-solving,*
> *communication, and group dynamic skills. Most*
> *written comments from students were positive, with*
> *only a handful clamoring for more structure and*
> *validation from the instructor.*

Our own impressions and the data we have collected are consistent with the growing body of systematic research into the effectiveness of PBL. The data from C.B.'s and José's classroom research, for instance, point to some of the strengths of PBL that have been confirmed by more formal inquiries: PBL students report satisfaction with the process, they attend class more regularly, and they express greater interest in courses and course materials (Banta, Black, & Kline, 2000). Our own experiences with examinations and other forms of evaluation of student performance are also mirrored in the evaluation research which has found that PBL students not only perform as well as traditional students, but they also retain information and transfer their learning more effectively (Banta, Black, & Kline, 2000; Edens, 2000; Hung, Bailey, & Jonassen, 2003).

The feedback we have received from students is more consistently positive than other reports of frustration at unclear assignments and a sense on the part of some students that they learned less or covered less than their peers in other, more traditional settings (see Banta, Black, & Kline, 2000; Edens, 2000; Lieux, 2001). However, we have heard some of these same criticisms.

Indeed, many of our suggestions for authoring problems, for pacing PBL activities, and for providing feedback and support are responses to the concerns of students.

It is difficult to make a definitive statement about the sustainability of PBL as an instructional strategy. For us, it has become a regular feature of our courses. Others, however, have tried it once or twice before returning to more traditional methods. Our best advice returns us to where we began. If you find yourself frustrated and perplexed when outstanding students are at a loss to remember and use the knowledge they have gained in class to solve an authentic problem, PBL is a strategy worth trying. If you craft good problems, develop the guiding skills necessary to nurture productive group work, manage the unstructured nature of a PBL classroom, and develop an evaluation strategy to balance group and individual contributions, PBL can be an effective learning tool. Whether you and your students think so will be up to you.

# Appendix 5.1
# Role Models? You Decide

## A Story of a Student Work Group

Some years ago, students in Professor Miles's Writing & Rhetoric 227 class were working together on group projects about midway through the semester. Professor Miles had placed them into four-person groups that she thought would work well together, based on what she knew about each student's strengths in the class so far.

The project—designing an interactive informational kiosk for use somewhere on campus—was important, worth 20% of their total grade. The assignment sheet said that the students needed to identify a place on campus that would benefit from an electronic kiosk, then decide what information to include and how, then to design a prototype. The project would last three weeks and end in a "sales pitch" presentation to the entire class. The entire group would receive the same grade.

### Meeting One: In Class

Professor Miles placed the following students in Group 3: Abigail, Chandra, Chuck, and Jerry. They had been given the assignment sheet and were urged to exchange contact information: phone, cell phone, email, and instant messaging (IM) addresses. They read their information aloud to each other, as each wrote it in their course notebooks. Jerry and Abigail joked that "Group 3" was a particularly bad name for their group, and they should find a better one. The group spent the next 20 minutes trying to come up with a name they all liked. By the end of the class session, all four agreed on *Nobody's Biz* as their group name. Class ended, and they went their separate ways.

## Meeting Two: In Class

When the class met again, Professor Miles began by asking the groups to report their two top contenders for kiosk location and audience. Groups 1 and 2 shared some interesting ideas, but *Nobody's Biz* was getting nervous because they had not even discussed that part of the assignment yet. When it was their turn, Chandra spoke for them and offered two ideas she had thought of herself: a parking lot kiosk that would indicate where spaces might be available, or an order-out menu kiosk for the dorms.

Given the chance to keep working on the project in class, *Nobody's Biz* thanked Chandra for saving them and offered support for her suggestions. They began working on them right away. Jerry agreed to contact local restaurants to get a comprehensive list of who delivers food into the dorms. Abigail signed up to survey dorm dwellers to see if they would take advantage of a new service like this. Chuck said he would try to find good examples of kiosks they could use as a model. Chandra asked about the other idea—the parking lot guide—and the group said she could start looking into that with her own research. They agreed to meet again during the next class and show what they'd done for homework.

## Meeting Three: In Class

Abigail was 20 minutes late to class; she couldn't find a parking space. Jerry didn't show up at all. Chuck was there, but hadn't had a chance to find any examples of kiosks, so he didn't have anything to show the group. Without Jerry and Abigail, Chandra and Chuck started discussing Chandra's work on the parking situation. They discussed locations for the kiosk and the possibility for wireless technologies to help the kiosks communicate with one another when the lots had filled. But who would input that information? And how would drivers know it was accurate? Chandra and Chuck were starting to think that perhaps they should return to the dorm food idea, when Abigail showed up—breathless and very annoyed. Parking, she said, was the single biggest thing wrong with this college, and they should do everything they could to make the situation better. With this new burst of energy, the group once again divided responsibilities to design a parking lot kiosk.

As class ended, Professor Miles reminded everyone that they had only two class sessions left before their final presentations. The groups that were meeting outside of class were significantly farther along in their ideas and designs, she said. *Nobody's Biz* decided to meet the next day in the library. Abigail volunteered to contact Jerry.

## Meeting Four: In the Library

Chandra arrived at 3:55 p.m., five minutes early for their group meeting. Chuck was right on time, but seemed distracted by his cell phone and kept exchanging text messages with somebody. Abigail showed up ten minutes late, with apologies for not being able to contact Jerry; her email to him had bounced back, and the cell phone number he'd given was a wrong number. It appeared they had no way to contact him. They decided not to tell Professor Miles, because they didn't want to get Jerry in trouble. Besides, he was still working on the dorm food project, and they'd decided to tackle parking availability.

During their time in the library, they read through each other's information, began putting it together, and argued about what the organization and design of the kiosk should be. Abigail felt very strongly that it should direct drivers to where they might find open spaces in each lot. Chuck rolled his eyes and questioned the feasibility of being able to do that. Trying to be diplomatic, Chandra asked Abigail to research that for the group to find out if it was possible. Chuck agreed to start designing the opening screen and figure out the menu, and Chandra was to start writing the persuasive part of the presentation—their script.

## Meeting Five: In Class

Chuck called before class to say he was sick, but asked Chandra to keep him posted on what they were doing in class. He said he'd be checking his email, and if they could get access to IM, he'd try to join with them in class from home. Abigail got the classroom IM up and running so they could include Chuck in the conversation, but he kept disappearing (maybe to get sick?), and the conversation stalled. Chuck assured them, however, that he had the design well underway.

Abigail, meanwhile, unveiled her plan for managing the parking space issue: repave each lot with sensors underneath, so the kiosk would receive that information and direct drivers exactly to where they would find empty spots. Chandra doubted that would ever be implemented by the college and wished Chuck were there to play devil's advocate. Chandra decided not to say anything negative to Abigail, and instead redirected the conversation to the script she was writing for the presentation. Several sections were missing the feasibility of their plan, and an implementation schedule and a persuasive pitch to the university administration to consider funding this initiative—one that was growing prohibitively costly with Abigail's sensor/repaving plan—were also needed.

They agreed to meet that afternoon in the parking lot to look around, get more ideas, and distribute some surveys.

## Meeting Six: In the Parking Lot

Chuck and Chandra arrived at the parking lot and immediately saw many problems with Abigail's sensor/repaving plan. Before Abigail arrived, they started figuring out how to scale back the kiosk so it would merely direct drivers to another lot if they couldn't find spaces here. The interactive portion of the kiosk would be a printout map to help them find other potential places to park. When Abigail arrived to hear this conversation, she was furious. Their revised plan would only send drivers around to other lots that might also be full! Chuck fought back that her plan was so impossible and ridiculous they'd be laughed out of class *and* they would all get a low grade on the project. He took a stand, refusing to do any more work until Abigail found an alternative to sensor paving—something she hadn't yet proven even existed. He got in his car and drove away, and Abigail did the same. Chandra stood alone in the lot, despairing that she hadn't been put in Group 2, holding the empty surveys in her hand.

## Meeting Seven: In Class

Sitting in class, there was Jerry! As promised, he had contacted all the local restaurants and gathered a list of everyone who delivered food to the dorms, or was hoping to implement such service in the future. Still angry with Abigail, Chuck didn't berate Jerry for dropping out. Instead, he challenged Abigail to unveil her new plan or offer proof of sensor paving. Hurt, Abigail said they should just forget it and go back to the dorm food delivery idea. Chandra quietly agreed, and Chuck fell silent. After another five minutes had passed, they all decided that with Jerry's information, the dorm food delivery system was probably a better project. For the rest of the class period, they tried to reconstruct the work they had done a few weeks before and assigned everyone new jobs to do before meeting to draft and design the final presentation in Chandra's dorm room the next night.

## Meeting Eight: Chandra's Dorm Room

No Jerry, but they did have the information he'd brought to class. Abigail was there, but didn't have the heart to participate beyond running out for munchies and soda with extra caffeine. So Chandra sat at her computer and composed the speech, while Chuck sat on a bed with his laptop and mocked up a PowerPoint version of their kiosk. Nobody spoke; the only sounds were some munching and the tapping of keyboards. Abigail sat on a rug on the floor while the other two worked, and eventually went home at 10:30. Chuck started to print out his slides, but then fell asleep. Chandra drafted an eight-page persuasive speech for the group to deliver the next morning. At 6:00, she woke up Chuck and told him to proofread the slides before going home to clean up, then she took a quick nap. They both hoped Jerry would show up.

## Meeting Nine: The In-Class Presentation

All four members of *Nobody's Biz* arrived wearing professional-looking clothes, and took turns talking about different stages of the project. Abigail introduced the overall concept, and Jerry spoke about the local restaurants' willingness to participate and maybe even bankroll part of the project. Chandra talked about implementation, and Chuck demonstrated how the kiosk would look using a PowerPoint prototype. The in-class audience was enthusiastic about the idea and said they'd love it if the college would do something like that.

## Result:

Every member of *Nobody's Biz* received an A on the project.

## You decide:

- Was this the right ending to the story?
- Is this a model for how you want your group to work?
- What went well?
- What went wrong?
- What guidelines will you draft to avoid their troubles?

*Note.* Adapted from Case Study: A College Classroom Discussion Group, originally published in Cragan, J. F., & Wright, D. W. (1986). *Communication in small group discussion: An integrated approach.* St. Paul, MN: West.

# Appendix 5.2
## Performance Evaluation
## NRS 212 Introduction to Soil Science

Student Evaluated _____ Problem _____

1. Did the person attend all class meetings, come prepared for the discussion, and contribute to the group's discussion?

| Never | Seldom | Sometimes | Often | Always |
|-------|--------|-----------|-------|--------|
| (0.70) | (0.80) | (0.90) | (1.00) | (1.05) |
| ☐ | ☐ | ☐ | ☐ | ☐ |

2. Did the person ask relevant questions and respond to the questions of others?

| Never | Seldom | Sometimes | Often | Always |
|-------|--------|-----------|-------|--------|
| (0.70) | (0.80) | (0.90) | (1.00) | (1.05) |
| ☐ | ☐ | ☐ | ☐ | ☐ |

3. Was the person willing to do work outside of class and bring relevant information back to the group for discussion?

| Never | Seldom | Sometimes | Often | Always |
|-------|--------|-----------|-------|--------|
| (0.70) | (0.80) | (0.90) | (1.00) | (1.05) |
| ☐ | ☐ | ☐ | ☐ | ☐ |

4. Was the person a good listener who respected the opinions of others?

| Never | Seldom | Sometimes | Often | Always |
|-------|--------|-----------|-------|--------|
| (0.70) | (0.80) | (0.90) | (1.00) | (1.05) |
| ☐ | ☐ | ☐ | ☐ | ☐ |

5. Did the person contribute to overall organization and group consensus?

| Never | Seldom | Sometimes | Often | Always |
|-------|--------|-----------|-------|--------|
| (0.70) | (0.80) | (0.90) | (1.00) | (1.05) |
| ☐ | ☐ | ☐ | ☐ | ☐ |

Comments:

*Note.* Adapted from Kitto, S. L., & Griffiths, L. G. (2001). The evolution of problem-based learning in a biotechnology course. In B. J. Duch, S. E. Groh, & D. E. Allen (Eds.), *The power of problem-based learning: A practical "how to" for teaching undergraduate courses in any discipline* (pp. 121–130). Sterling, VA: Stylus.

# Epilogue

Beginning with its introduction in medical schools, problem-based learning has slowly worked its way into more and more of the nation's higher education classrooms. Although the natural sciences probably continue to offer more PBL opportunities than the social sciences, the arts, and the humanities, faculty in the "softer" disciplines are no longer strangers to PBL practices. As PBL becomes part of the instructional repertoire of faculty throughout the university, its capacity to encourage deep learning, foster collaboration, and immerse students in authentic problems will appear in various disciplines and at various levels of the curricula. As familiarity and comfort with the practice of PBL grows, we expect that faculty will find new and creative ways to employ the sequence of collaborative discovery and reflection that lies at the heart of the method. There are, to be sure, many classroom uses of PBL that have yet to be explored, and we hope this book will encourage our colleagues to take on some of that work.

The promise of PBL is not, however, limited to the transforming effects it has on classroom instruction. The basic PBL structure of "what do we know, what do we need to know, how can we learn it" also offers a foundation for building robust assessments of student learning outcomes in both departmental and university-wide contexts. The activities embedded in the practice of PBL are especially well suited for the creation of authentic assessments that ask students to use (rather than merely recall) what they have learned to address and analyze an issue of some import.

We are not the first to see that the practices of PBL and assessment of student learning fit neatly together. In 1996, the now-defunct American Association for Higher Education (AAHE) articulated "Nine Principles of Good Practice for Assessing Student Learning" that stressed, among other things, that effective assessment was based on the understanding of "learning as multidimensional, integrated, and revealed in performance over time" (Maki, 2004, p. 23). Further, the AAHE panel noted that assessment "requires attention to outcomes but also and equally to the experiences that lead to those outcomes" (Maki, p. 23) and they emphasized that assessment will make a difference when it "begins with issues of use and illuminates questions that people really care about" (Maki, p. 24). The features of "good assessment practice" resemble nothing so much as the features of an effective, engaging PBL session.

There are several aspects of PBL that make adapting it to assessment worth thinking about. First, good PBL problems are authentic, derived from real circumstances that engage students not merely as course requirements but because the situation matters as something "people really care about." Second, PBL demands that students demonstrate their ability to employ concepts, frame appropriate questions, and collect and analyze data in ways that go well beyond the superficial recitation of information. Third, PBL requires that students work collaboratively with others, a skill increasingly identified as essential for productive, satisfying careers. Finally, PBL problems are easily adapted to multi- or cross-disciplinary settings. Posing an engaging, multidisciplinary problem that requires students to use what they have learned in collaboration with others is one way to imagine an authentic assessment of the student outcomes of a general education curriculum.

The Indian Ocean tsunami problem mentioned in Chapter 3 helps to illustrate the capacity of PBL to become a comprehensive assessment instrument. The tsunami and its consequences could be fashioned into a problem that asked students to think simultaneously along scientific, political, economic, medical, and ethical dimensions. Creating groups of students—perhaps mixing biology majors with philosophy majors, or natural resource science majors with anthropology majors—asking them to develop plans to alleviate the current suffering and policies to lessen the probability of future tragedies, would create a context for assessing not only students' academic accomplishments, but also their ability to work with others as thoughtful and engaged citizens.

Obviously there is much yet to do if the tsunami problem (or any PBL problem) is to become an effective and reliable measure of students' learning—a product would have to be specified, rubrics would need to be constructed, group and individual accomplishments would need to be untangled—but the promise is clearly there. PBL offers a unique setting for students to identify what they know; inquire about what they do not; collect, analyze, and evaluate information; and present what they have learned to others. In short, PBL allows both us and our students to see the purpose of higher education in action: informed, thoughtful, and engaged citizens working together to solve problems that people really care about.

# Bibliography

Albanese, M. A., & Mitchell, S. (1993, January). Problem-based learning: A review of literature on its outcomes and implementation issues. *Academic Medicine, 68*(1), 52–81.

Allen, R., & Rooney, P. (1998, June). Designing a problem-based learning environment for ESL students in business communication. *Business Communication Quarterly, 61*(2), 48–56.

Amador, J. A., & Görres, J. H. (2004). A problem-based learning approach to teaching introductory soil science. *Journal of Natural Resources and Life Sciences Education, 33,* 21–27.

Banta, T. W., Black, K. E., & Kline, K. A. (2000). PBL 2000 plenary address offers evidence for and against problem-based learning. *PBL Insight, 3*(3). Retrieved February 7, 2006, from www.samford.edu/pubs/pbl/pbl3.3.pdf

Boud, D., & Feletti, G. (Eds.). (1997). *The challenge of problem-based learning* (2nd ed.). London, England: Kogan Page.

Daiute, C., & Dalton, B. (1993). Collaboration between children learning to write: Can novices be masters? *Cognition and Instruction, 10,* 281–333.

Delisle, R. (1997). *How to use problem-based learning in the classroom.* Alexandria, VA: Association for Supervision and Curriculum Development.

Dominowski, R. L. (1998). Verbalization and problem solving. In D. J. Hacker, J. Dunlosky, & A. C. Graesser (Eds.), *Metacognition in educational theory and practice* (pp. 25–36). Hillsdale, NJ: Erlbaum.

Duch, B. J., Groh, S. E., & Allen, D. E. (Eds.). (2001). *The power of problem-based learning: A practical "how to" for teaching undergraduate courses in any discipline.* Sterling, VA: Stylus.

Edens, K. M. (2000). Preparing problem solvers for the 21st century through problem-based learning. *College Teaching, 48*(2), 55–60.

Erickson, B. L., Peters, C. B., & Strommer, D. W. (2006). *Teaching first-year college students.* San Francisco: Jossey-Bass.

Horowitz, D. (2001, January 3). *Ten reasons why reparations for blacks is a bad idea for blacks—and racist too.* Retrieved February 7, 2006, from www.frontpagemag.com/Articles/ReadArticle.asp?ID=1153

Hung, W., Bailey, J. H., & Jonassen, D. H. (2003). Exploring the tensions of problem-based learning: Insights from research. In D. S. Knowlton & D. C. Sharp (Eds.), *New directions in teaching and learning: No. 95. Problem-based learning in the Information Age* (pp. 13–24). San Francisco, CA: Jossey-Bass.

Johnson, D. W., Johnson, R. T., & Smith, K. A. (1991). *Active learning: Cooperation in the college classroom.* Edina, MN: Interaction Book Company.

Lieux, E. M. (2001). A skeptic's look at PBL. In B. J. Duch, S. E. Groh, & D. E. Allen (Eds.), *The power of problem-based learning: A practical "how to" for teaching undergraduate courses in any discipline* (pp. 13–24). Sterling, VA: Stylus.

Maki, P. L. (2004). *Assessing for learning: Building a sustainable commitment across the institution.* Sterling, VA: Stylus.

Neufeld, V. R., & Barrows, H. S. (1974, November). The "McMaster philosophy": An approach to medical education. *Journal of Medical Education, 49*(11), 1040–1050.

Porter, J. E., Sullivan, P., & Johnson-Eilola, J. (2003). *Professional writing online, version 2.0* (2nd ed.). New York, NY: Longman.

Robinson, R. (2000). *The debt: What America owes to blacks.* New York, NY: Dutton.

Sommers, N. (1982). Responding to student writing. *College Composition and Communication, 33*(2), 148–156.

Sommers, N. (1992). Between the drafts. *College Composition and Communication, 43*(1), 23–31.

Tyler, A. (2001). *Back when we were grownups.* New York, NY: Ballantine Books.

Williams, B. (2001). The theoretical links between problem-based learning and self-directed learning for continuing professional nursing education. *Teaching in Higher Education, 6*(1), 85–98.

Woods, D. R. (1996). Problem-based learning for large classes in chemical engineering. In L. Wilkerson & W. H. Gijselaers (Eds.), *New directions for teaching and learning: No. 68. Bringing problem-based learning to higher education: Theory and practice* (pp. 91–100). San Francisco, CA: Jossey-Bass.

# Index